SHADOW QUILTS

Easy-to-Design Multiple Image Quilts

Patricia Maixner Magaret
Donna Ingram Slusser

C&T PUBLISHING

DL ᴴᴮ Ľ Vwm

Copyright © 2000 by Patricia Maixner Magaret and Donna Ingram Slusser

Editor: Cyndy Lyle Rymer
Technical Editor: Carolyn Aune
Copy Editor: Vera Tobin
Cover, Book Design, and Illustrations: Aliza Kahn
Design Direction: Diane Pedersen
Front Cover Photo: "Jewel Box," original design by Carol Honderich, Goshen, Indiana; interpretation by Donna Ingram Slusser, Pullman, Washington, 1999, 41" x 41".
Back Cover Photo: "Pinwheels Spinning," designed and machine quilted by Donna Ingram Slusser, Pullman, Washington; top made by Kirstin Linnett Nicholson, Seaback, Washington, 1999, 50" square.
Photography: Mark Frey. Photo on page 76 by Sharon Risedorph.

Attention Teachers:
C&T Publishing, Inc. encourages you to use this book as a text for teaching. Contact us at 800-284-1114 or www.ctpub.com for more information about the C&T Teachers Program.

Trademarked (™) and Registered Trademarked (®) names are used throughout this book. Rather than use the symbols with every occurrence of a trademark and registered trademark name, we have only used the symbol the first time the product appears. We are using the names only in an editorial fashion and to the benefit of the owner, with no intention of infringement.

Library of Congress Cataloging-in-Publication Data

Magaret, Pat Maixner
    Shadow quilts : easy to design multiple image quilts / Patricia
Maixner Magaret, Donna Ingram Slusser.
    p. cm.
  Includes index.
  ISBN 1-57120-093-2 (paper trade)
  1. Strip quilting Patterns. 2. Patchwork Patterns. I. Slusser,
Donna Ingram, II. Title.
  TT835 .M27145 1999
  746.46'041--dc21
                        99-6788
                        CIP
Published by C&T Publishing, Inc.
P.O. Box 1456
Lafayette, California 94549

Printed in Hong Kong
10   9   8   7   6   5   4   3   2   1

Contents

Dedication 5

Acknowledgments 5

Introduction 6

Chapter 1:
Multiple Image Design 9
How to Use This Book.................................9
Terms and Definitions.................................10
Let's Get Started...14

Chapter 2:
Designing a Shadow Quilt..................17
Selecting the Original Block...........................17
Designing a Shadow Quilt 20
Drawing the Individual Blocks Layer.................21
Drawing the Shadow Layer 22

Chapter 3:
From Our Stash................................25
Contrast..25
Getting It All Together 34
Color Inspiration 34

Chapter 4:
Spread Your Wings and Fly 39
Theme and Variations 39
Mystery—The Case of the Lost Shadow............40
Mystery—The Case of Which Way
        Did They Go?.....................................44
Mystery—The Case of the Line-Up 46
Mystery—The Case of the Rebellious Blocks.....49
Mystery—The Case of the
        See-Through Shadow 52
Mystery—The Case of the Wanted Poster 54
Good Detectives 55

Chapter 5: Mock-Up Magic...................57
Supplies 57
Make a Mock-Up...58

Chapter 6: High-Tech Design 63
Quilt Design Software....................................64
Drawing Software...66

Chapter 7:
General Project Guidelines.................69
Accurate Piecing 69
Fabric Requirements 69
Fabric Grain 69
Pressing 69
No-Template Method for Cutting Triangles.......70
Borders 70
Binding..73
Hanging Sleeve 75
Labels 75

Projects 76
Shoo-Fly Don't Bother Me 76
Shadow Play...79
Fire and Ice..82
Jewel Box...85
A Dash Through the Garden 88
Rainbow Stars...91
Autumn Leaves: A Shadow Quilt 96
Pinwheels Spinning 100
Passing Through 104

Sources...109

Index 110

About the Authors 111

PINWHEELS...WHEELS...WHEELS
Marje Rhine
Boring, Oregon, 1998
65" x 65"

A collection of scrappy light-colored fabrics is a

backdrop for three layers of pinwheels. The center

gold and medium green Shadows serve as a nice

contrast for the smaller, randomly placed pinwheels.

Dedication

To Anna, my personal angel in Heaven. Your life may have been short, but you have given me the strength to follow my dreams and search for new horizons. I see you in every sunrise, every blooming flower and fluttering butterfly. I miss you. Mom (Patricia)

To Lloyd, the fantastic finder of lost things, the super chef, and the endless encourager: your gentle nature and deep spirit bring light to the shadows in my life. Donna

Acknowledgments

Thanks to Lloyd, the superintendent of "mock-up magic." Without your dedicated hours with sticky fingers, this book wouldn't have happened. Hope you got caught up on your westerns at the same time.

Thanks to the students and friends who made quilts for this project. This book would not have been possible without all of your masterpieces. Each one of you is a special and talented quiltmaker who was willing to share.

Thanks to our friends. We apologize for missing meetings and shirking other duties and responsibilities while writing this book. Yet you have stood by us and offered your help in any possible way. Your encouraging words have been invaluable.

Thanks to Cyndy Rymer, Carolyn Aune, Aliza Kahn, Diane Pedersen and the expert staff at C&T Publishing. Your help, advice and confidence in us has made the writing of *Shadow Quilts* a fun adventure.

Thanks to Cheryl Swain and Pam Clarke, accomplished machine quilting experts. For Patricia, time was tight, but you enthusiastically agreed to help her finish her quilts. Your work is beautiful.

Thanks to Terry Huhta, the computer wizard of the Palouse. We appreciate your time and effort to help us check our math and methods (and maybe our madness, too!).

Thanks to Mark Frey, assistant amateur quilt-namer and caption writer, but more importantly, master photographer. Every quilt that passed your camera lens, your eagle eye, and magic methods all turned out "primo." We had lots of fun, too.

Thanks to Marna Bobb, the silhouette queen of the Pullman School District. We will always value the cuttings that you did of our children when they were in your kindergarten class. Thanks for agreeing to do ours, too. We appreciate the curly eyelashes and classy coifed "do's." We'll make an appointment for the doggies soon.

Thanks to Mom, Lois Ingram, for your patience, help, and our glorious spring walks during the final weeks of manuscript madness. With much gratitude, Mom. Donna

Thanks to our families. You have been with us through thick and thin.

Thanks to Abby, Bailey, and Lily, the distributors of soft and comforting "puppy fur." You helped us by insisting that we get outside daily to observe Mother Nature in all her glory.

Introduction

From the minute we entered this world, we imagine that we both came out kicking and crying, "Where is some light? We need sunshine! Let us smell a rose!" We both appreciate all aspects of nature. As babies, we preferred the colors of the bouquet of flowers on the dining room table to the mobile dancing over our cribs. The outdoors beckoned to us. Our mothers took us on buggy rides and introduced us to the very tall trees, the cool refreshing grass (which didn't taste very good), and to the ever-so-big blue sky, the sun, moon, and stars.

We began to explore our world by ourselves, and when we learned to walk we found there was always someone nearby who looked just like us, only it was a dark shape. When we wanted her to leave us alone, she refused to go. It was always such fun to play with our shadow friend—to jump on her, to put her behind us when we felt strong, or to have her lead the way into a scary situation. Patricia named her shadow Camille, the sister she never had.

On dark days we could not understand why our shadows did not come out to play. We thought they must be scared of the dark or didn't want to get wet in the rain. Patricia remembers asking her mother where shadows came from. The answer was always, "When you or another object block the rays of light, a dark shadow is formed."

We remember family gatherings when we were children. Donna's family had frequent get-togethers, and everyone brought their home movies and slides to show after a big, wonderful meal. With our tummies full, we often snoozed through the travel portions of the movies and slides, but woke up when it was time to change the reels or slide trays. It was during these interludes that Dad Ingram taught Donna, her brothers, and all the cousins how to make finger shadows in the projector's light. What fun to learn how to make a shadow rabbit and watch its ears wiggle, or to create a dog and see it's mouth open and close as we tried to coordinate our "woof-woof" with our fingers. Patricia remembers making shadow animal shapes on the wall with her friends and family. They would take turns making the animals while the others had to guess which one it was.

In the summer before third grade, Donna and her brother, David, started picking berries in the Willamette Valley farms near their home. They would rise at the crack of dawn to ride their bikes to the strawberry or raspberry fields. In the chilly early morning light, they watched their shadow feet quickly pedal the extra-long bike shadows to keep pace with the riders who were pedaling fast to keep warm. They saw long shadows form in the valleys as the sun peeked over the hilltops. After picking berries until mid-afternoon (and probably eating as many as they picked), they pedaled their bikes home. Funny how the bike shadows were not as big during this time of day, and the shadows in the valleys were very short.

During those growing-up years we were constantly reminded of shadows. We sat with our ears glued to the old radio program, "The Shadow," and faithfully listened to each week's adventure. Recently, we enjoyed watching the movie adventures of our radio hero, Lamar Cranston. The radio still plays renditions of "Me and My Shadow," a popular tune about these elusive shapes.

In school we found the answers to some of our early questions about shadows. In science class we learned that the higher the sun is in the sky, the shorter the shadow. The lower the sun, the longer the shadow. We learned the theory for why winter shadows are longer than those of summer. Patricia remembers a geometry test question: Determine the length of your shadow (indicating your height) at 2 pm on June 14th of any given year. It was hard to resist answering: "There was no shadow because it was cloudy that day." She knew that the teacher would not appreciate the easy answer.

Donna forgot about her childhood adventures with shadows until she was visiting her son and daughter-in-law, Larry and Nicole, and their two-year-old daughter, Hannah Victoria Slusser. On a brisk December morning, grandmother and granddaughter went for a walk and ended up dancing with their shadows. They giggled as they watched their attached shapes huff and puff and blow big breaths of frosty, cold air. They laughed at nothing and laughed at everything as they ran fast, ran slow, and waved their arms in the air. Two real people sang and joined hands with two shadows and played Ring Around the Rosy. What a reflective moment for Donna, as she recaptured some of her lost innocence that morning and found joy as she remembered and took delight in life's simple things.

We both became quilters in the early 1980s. We became friends as well as business partners while team-teaching a color class for quilters. It is amazing that we can work together because we use different techniques and methods for almost everything, and our creative processes are complete opposites. Patricia is the template queen while Donna prefers no-template methods when using the rotary cutter. Patricia puts her ideas down on graph paper. Donna is a visualizer who can go from ideas and pictures in her mind directly to cutting fabric. Patricia is orderly, methodical, and accomplishes tasks in a timely manner. Donna tends to fly by the seat of her pants, and loves to skip from step one to step four, then back to steps two and three if necessary. We have learned to appreciate and celebrate our differences because we each have a commitment to good workmanship, no matter what technique is used.

Our students usually identify with one of us, or some say they have a combination of both of us in them. We hope our differences encourage you to find the techniques that work best for you, as well as lead you on a discovery of your own creative means of expression.

When we entered the world of quiltmaking, we both started with traditional patterns and soon found ourselves tampering with hard-set rules and pushing our designs in new directions. One of Patricia's first departures from strict tradition was the design of a Christmas quilt based on the Barbara Fritchie Star block. This quilt could be appreciated on two levels. When viewed up close, many individual stars were visible, but when you stepped back, a large star emerged in the background—a star that "shadowed" the others. It became apparent that this design technique could be used with other block patterns. In 1994, we both began playing with this fun design technique. Our friends asked us to teach them how to create these designs; another class was born and we began teaching it in our travels. Students had so much fun and experienced so much freedom using this process that a book was soon in the works. When we first started seriously designing Shadow Quilts, graph paper and pencils filled our drawers. Now our computers with their quilt design and draw programs are taking over our lives. Modern technology is making our design process easier and faster. Our grandmothers would be jealous. However, the simple aspects of our existence remain a constant reminder to help us keep our lives in perspective—whether it be the cool grass, a tall tree, the sky, the sun, the moon, and the stars, the good Lord above, or shadows.

Join us in another step on our quiltmaking journey as we explore new horizons and dimensions in creating Shadow Quilts.

AUTUMN ACCENTS
Donna Ingram Slusser
Pullman, Washington, 1998
59" x 59"

Multicolored leaves swoop and swish while performing their

autumn dance against a golden Shadow. The swirling wind

quilting lines add to the atmosphere and illusion of motion.

CHAPTER 1

Multiple Image Design

Shadow Quilts are beautiful, one-of-a-kind quilts. They look complex, but are relatively easy to design. Most are based on blocks with simple shapes, making them easy to piece. Each design can be as simple or as complicated as you wish.

Shadow Quilts use several layers of images to make a design. The smaller, individual blocks make up one layer. The Shadow layer is a larger image that usually resides in the background of the smaller blocks. Sometimes there are additional levels in the design when blocks of multiple sizes are included. One layer catches our attention first because it is easily visible, while another layer may be more secretive and hidden.

When people view a Shadow Quilt, they first admire the overall design and the color scheme. Then a puzzled look will come over their face. There is something about the quilt that makes it different from a traditional quilt. After they ponder for a few moments, a smile will come over their face, their eyes will light up, and they'll say, "Aha, I discovered something the quiltmaker has hidden in the design."

Are you a quiltmaker who would like to "spread your design wings" ? The Shadow Quilt technique is a good way to begin. The basic method teaches you some simple concepts, then the ideas and "what ifs" come so rapidly you'll have a hard time deciding which one to pursue.

If you are more experienced with the design process, you will love the challenge of experimenting with design, color, and fabrics.

Because these quilts look complex, there is an "intimidation factor" that scares some quilters. As the students come through the door into our classroom, you can see the trepidation on their faces and hear them say to themselves, "I'm not quite sure why I'm here." We begin the class with a teaching trunk show. We point out the layers containing the individual blocks and ask students to find the shadows, or reverse the visual clues. Soon you can see the creativity start to flow as they begin to think about their own designs.

How to Use This Book

Shadow Quilts encourage our detective powers. Good detectives conduct an investigation to find answers. They might even go undercover to shadow or follow someone to gain information that will help them solve the case. Why don't we gather our Quilter's Gumshoe Tools to use while we learn about Shadow Quilts? Our super-sleuth equipment is a magnifying glass to use when searching for clues and a key to help unlock the mysteries and puzzles. A big pay-off of creative ideas comes when the mystery is solved. These symbols are scattered throughout the book to aid our investigation.

The material is presented in a methodical manner — each concept builds on the previously presented material. Read this chapter to find clues about terms and definitions. There are references to specific quilts to help point the way. Next turn to Chapter 2 to learn which blocks to use and how to draw a simple Shadow Quilt. The next chapter, *From Our Stash*, gives tips about which fabrics to use in Shadow Quilts. Then travel to *Spread Your Wings and Fly* where you'll find lots of mysteries, puzzles, clues, keys, and big payoffs! You'll also find ideas about where to look for inspiration for a variety of wonderful color schemes:

FOREST FOR THE TREES
Sally Schneider,
Breinigsville, Pennsylvania, 1998
81" x 81"

Sally's forest of colorful trees has been turned

on point and placed over the dark green

Shadow. The subtle border fabric provides the

perfect frame.

they can be smashing, exciting, or tranquil, as suits your mood.

What if you don't want to make another quilt, since your beds and cupboards are already overflowing? Or maybe you want to audition your color scheme and fabrics. *Mock-Up Magic* shows you how to make a model that can be framed to hang on your wall. *High-Tech Design* discusses computer software programs. Some of us had to be dragged kicking and screaming into cyberspace. But once we got there, we wondered how we ever got along without e-mail, drawing programs, and quilt design software. The nine projects at the back of the book will help you get started.

As you peruse this book, we hope you chase your shadow, wave your arms, watch your shadow dance, and try "what ifs." Experience wonder when you see the design emerging. Most of all, play and have fun.

Terms and Definitions

⊙━ Multi-Layer Designs

One of the most intriguing features of Shadow Quilts is the fact that they can be viewed and appreciated on several different levels. How many layers are in a Shadow Quilt? Look for the different design elements. There are small individual blocks that make up one layer. A larger image, the Shadow, is on a different level. If we imagine stacking transparent pieces of film with the Shadow drawn on one of them, and the layer containing the individual blocks on the other, the result is this two-layer design. Either the Shadow or the individual blocks can be transparent or opaque, depending on the effect you want. In Sally Schneider's "Forest for the Trees" we can easily see the two layers of the design. The small trees are placed in a traditional on-point quilt setting to make up one layer, while the larger Shadow tree resides in the background layer.

TOO MANY STARS
Carolyn Fiscus Gottschalk
Viola, Idaho, 1998
48" x 48"

The shadow is subtle in this variable star quilt. The variation of star sizes gives the illusion and depth. Fractured stars add interest.

UNTITLED 5
Barbara H. McDowell
San Diego, California, 1999
38" x 38"

The high contrast of the warm/cool color scheme creates a sharp, crisp feeling that is softened by the graceful, curved quilting lines. The corner triangle units move the eye toward the exciting center.

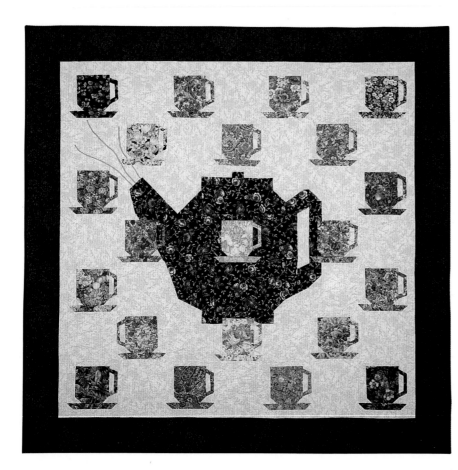

MY CUP OF TEA
Donna Ingram Slusser
Pullman, Washington, 1999
50" x 50"

Donna enjoys giving tea parties, collecting

teacups, and adding to her stash of floral fabrics.

This original design combines all three passions

and sets floral teacups between alternate

background blocks. Notice that there is one

teacup for a guest who is left-handed. Owned

by Hannah Slusser.

Sometimes multiple block sizes are used in the design, creating a third or even more layers. Carolyn Gottschalk's "Too Many Stars" (page 11) contains three layers. The smallest stars form a layer as they spread across the dark medium-size star layer, and the large, subtle gray Shadow unifies the design.

Basic Block

Choose a basic block for the design. Often the smaller, individual blocks and the Shadow are based on the same block. Sometimes the blocks are very familiar and traditional. Billie Mahorney's "Shoo Fly from Outer Space" (page 20) utilizes the very familiar Shoo-Fly block as the basis for her design. You may decide to change or adapt a traditional block. Patricia's "Passing Through" (page 104) is based on the Windblown Square block, even though it is difficult to recognize the traditional block pattern.

Sometimes the Shadow and the smaller, individual blocks are different, but the blocks are related by theme. "My Cup of Tea" by Donna uses two blocks—a teapot for the Shadow and teacups for small blocks.

Individual Blocks

Small, individual blocks make up one layer in the design. They are usually one pattern, as seen in "Untitled 5" by Barbara McDowell (page 11). There can also be a variety of individual block patterns relating to one another and the Shadow by theme. "Sew This Is What Quilting Is All About," an original design by Patricia and Donna (page 68), is a potpourri of small blocks that carry out the sewing machine Shadow theme.

Individual blocks can be put together in a style similar to a traditional setting: side by side or in an alternate plain block setting. For example, Donna chose to put plain blocks in between the basket blocks in "A Tisket a Tasket" in order to make the Shadow more visible.

A TISKET A TASKET
Donna Ingram Slusser
Pullman, Washington, 1999
76" x 76"

The spring palette of the small tulip baskets
is enhanced by the rich summer hues of
the Shadow.

The Shadow

You will form this layer by filling in some of the background space in your individual blocks. The larger image can be the same as the smaller blocks or selected from a variety of blocks.

True Shadow

This Shadow is a replica of the individual blocks and is usually the most easily recognized pattern. Even so, sometimes you need good sleuthing skills to find the Shadow. Donna's "Blue Plane Special" (page 35) is an example of two layers based on the same basic block with a Shadow that is easily seen. Patricia's "Phantom Fleet" (page 43) challenges you to find the large ghost ship.

Theme Shadow

Sometimes the Shadow relates to the individual blocks by theme. "Sew This Is What Quilting Is All About" (page 68) uses the Shadow sewing machine as the main theme block in the design and the individual blocks support this idea.

Transparent Shadow

Sometimes the Shadow is not in the background but appears like a transparent film on top of the original blocks. In Patricia's quilt "Fire and Ice" (page 82), a Shadow acts like a spotlight over the individual blocks. This effect is described beginning on page 52.

So which layer do we see first, the Shadow or the individual blocks? It depends on the design, the fabric choices, and the color scheme.

When viewing Becky Keck's "Star Shadows" (page 44), we first notice the blue Shadow. On closer examination, we discover smaller blocks of the same image scattered over the design. The quilt invites us to come closer to check for more clues. Hmmmm. Some blocks are missing while others have only partial pieces of the star. Interesting effect!

TRIPLE TROPICAL FRUIT
Sara Jane Perino
Pullman, Washington, 1999
32" x 32"

The visual complexity of this design is
actually simple when broken down into three
individual layers. The unusual combination of
tropical fruit colors suggests transparency.

Sometimes we see the layer containing the smaller, individual blocks first. "Triple Tropical Fruit" by Sara Jane Perino has many small stars placed over the background layer. As we search for other layers, our eyes focus on the stars that are two sizes—the pink-red layer and the golden-yellow layer.

Often, the blocks and designs on the different layers can be seen almost simultaneously, as in Ellis Farny's "Glorious Iris."

Can you see how the possibilities for Shadow Quilts are endless? You can make the design whatever you want it to be.

⊶ Grid System for Blocks

Blocks are generally based on a grid. The grid lines divide the block into individual units that are equal.

For example, a three-unit block is established on a grid with three units on each side.

3-unit grid

Shoo-Fly

Let's Get Started

We've always wanted to hop into a taxi and say, "Follow that car!" but haven't had a chance yet. So let's do it now. Grab that graph paper and find some sharp pencils or fire up the computer, turn the pages in these next chapters, and follow that Shadow!

GLORIOUS IRIS
Ellis R. Farny
La Mirada, California, 1998
55" x 55"

Ellis loves seasonal quilts and this one definitely says spring in California. Batik fabrics bring richness to the pieced block by Ruby McKim.

MOSAIC STAR
Shirley Perryman
Cary, North Carolina, 1998
50" x 50"

The Mosaic Star block becomes an eye-catching textured Shadow in this attractive quilt. Different size stars float on the layers and add to the dimensional appearance.

MANTILLA FOR MOM

Patricia Maixner Magaret, Pullman, Washington, 1999
Machine quilted by Pam Clarke, Spokane, Washington
67" x 67"

The delicate texture of the lacy Shadow fabric contrasts in an exciting fashion with the vibrant, unconventional color scheme. The individual Pinwheel Star blocks have been offset on the Shadow grid and parts of them omitted. The green pinwheels appear to be spinning in a ring around a circle of complete blocks. The angled borders are a perfect complement.

CHAPTER 2

Designing
A Shadow Quilt

A Shadow Quilt can be as simple or as complex as you want it to be. We will start with a few guidelines and a simple practice project. Then you can use your ideas to create original designs.

Selecting the Original Block

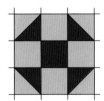 To select a block pattern for the design, you need to study potential blocks to see if they have characteristics that will work easily in a Shadow Quilt design. Consider the following:

• grid system
• basic shapes
• space, both positive and negative

⊙━ Block Grid System

Blocks are categorized using a "patch" system based on a grid. The square grid is most common, and the block is divided into individual, equal units. This grid will be the easiest to use for Shadow Quilts, at least in the beginning.

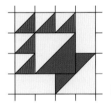

To determine a block's grid, count the number of units on one side of the block.

This Shoo-Fly block has three equal divisions on each side. Traditionally this is referred to as a nine-patch block. However, for the sake of simplicity and to avoid confusion, we will refer to the grid system for each block, using the exact number of units on one side of the grid. Thus, this is a three-unit block.

Generally speaking, the easiest blocks to use for Shadow Quilts are based on the three-unit or four-unit grid. The Shoo-Fly is an example of a three-unit block. The simple basket block is a good example of a four-unit block.

Four-unit basket block

Of course, there are always exceptions, and students come up with great designs using a five-, six-, or even seven-unit grid. "I Never Saw a Purple Bear" by Ellen Krieger (page 18) is based on a seven-unit grid.

⊙━ Shapes within the Block

Analyze the potential block. What are the basic shapes—squares, triangles, rectangles, diamonds, trapezoids? Simple shapes are the easiest to use when designing a Shadow Quilt.

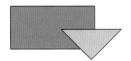

I NEVER SAW A PURPLE BEAR
Ellen Krieger
Summerville, Oregon, 1998
59" x 59"

A trail of bear tracks wend their way across a
purple Bear Paw Shadow. The background floral
fabric creates a nice contrast against the more
subtle fabrics in the design.

It is difficult to work with more complicated shapes because they require elaborate piecing when creating the Shadow layer of the design. Notice we said difficult, not impossible.

Parallelograms can be made from squares and half-square triangles. "Star Shadows" (page 44) illustrates how the quiltmaker used these shapes to create parallelograms.

Trapezoids can be made from squares and half-square triangles.

There are other ways to adapt a design when you want to use a complicated shape.

Quilters are good problem solvers. If your block of choice has an unusually shaped piece, don't immediately discard it. Consider it thoughtfully and try the possibilities. "Arcturus" is an example of a block with many unusual shapes. The quiltmaker created common lines between the individual blocks that unified the complete design. Look at the other quilts scattered throughout the book to see how others solved the challenges they encountered. Refer to the information in *Spread Your Wings and Fly* (page 39) for more ideas.

⚷ Space

Space is the total area of a design. Objects and images in the design take up space and are considered positive. The empty space between and around these images is called negative space.

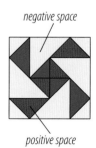

negative space

positive space

ARCTURAS
Virginia O'Donnell
Portland, Oregon, 1999
41" x 41"

Virginia was attracted to the block Virginia
Star from *The Quilter's Album of Blocks and
Borders* by Jinny Beyer. Arcturas is the fourth
brightest star in the sky and is an orange star
in the northern constellation Bootes. Because
of its characteristics it became the name of
this wallhanging.

For the Shadow to work, the basic block must have at least 50% negative space. The Shadow layer is created in the negative space of the small individual blocks. If there is not enough empty, negative space, the Shadow melds into the individual blocks and the design elements are lost.

  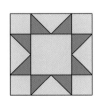

These blocks have a good balance between positive and negative space.

  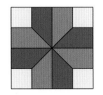

These blocks would be difficult to use for a Shadow Quilt design because they do not contain enough negative space.

Suppose you really, really want to use a block with little negative space. Don't despair. Options and examples are in *Spread Your Wings and Fly* (page 39). Check it out!

The Basic Block has:

- easy grid
- simple shapes
- at least 50% negative space

There are many blocks that meet the basic criteria shown in quilting resource books. In addition, some interesting blocks are shown on page 23 for your consideration.

SHOO FLY FROM OUTER SPACE
Billie Mahorney
Portland, Oregon, 1998
41" x 41"

The simple Shoo Fly pattern is exciting when
unique batik fabrics are chosen for their color
and texture. The addition of a simple pieced
border adds a nice frame. The subtle contrast
between the blocks and Shadow invites the
viewer to come up for a closer look. Project
instructions for a similar quilt begin on page 76.

Designing a Shadow Quilt

Supplies

Pencil; eraser; graph paper (4 or 8 squares per inch);
colored pencils—three strong, very different colors,
such as red, blue, and green.

Planning

Let's use a simple block,
the Shoo-Fly.

Step 1. Check the original block to see if it meets the
guidelines:

CRITERIA	SHOO-FLY
• easy grid	• three-patch
• simple shapes	• squares and triangles
• 50% negative space	• over 50% negative space

The Shoo-Fly block meets all of the basic criteria with
no adjustments needed.

Step 2. Determine the Shadow design. For this exercise, the Shadow is the same as the original—a large
Shoo-Fly block.

Step 3. Select the number of layers in the design. To
keep things simple, we will have only two layers—one
for the smaller individual blocks, the other for the
Shadow.

There are several ways to begin designing a Shadow
Quilt. Sometimes the Shadow level is drawn first, but
for this project, we will begin with the individual
blocks. No matter which layer is drawn first, the other
layer soon becomes a factor in the process. The technique can seem rather cumbersome at first, but after
learning the concept, your confidence will grow and
designing becomes easier.

Drawing the Individual Blocks Layer

We recommend using colored pencils that can be easily seen on graph paper, such as red, green, blue, purple, etc. Yellow and pale colors do not show up well. For this exercise, the illustrations use blue and green. Substitute other colors if you wish.

Step 1. Draw one Shoo-Fly block on graph paper (4 squares per inch). Each unit in the block is represented by one square on the graph paper. The Shoo-Fly block is based on a three-unit grid because there are three equal units on each side. Your drawing uses nine squares of graph paper.

Step 2. Color the shapes that make the Shoo-Fly design. Outline the block with a contrasting color. In the illustration the Shoo-Fly shapes were filled in blue and the block outlined in green.

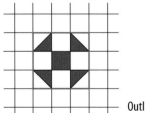

Outlined and filled-in block

Step 3. Shadow quilts obviously have more than one individual block in the plan. How many additional blocks are needed to make a complete design? The Shoo-Fly is a three-unit block and has a total of nine units, so our Shadow grid must also use this number of units. Begin drawing additional Shoo-Fly blocks, shading them in blue and outlining them in green, making sure that the blocks are right next to each other.

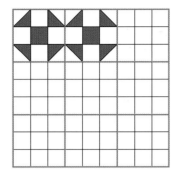

Adding more blocks

Step 4. Continue drawing, filling, and outlining blocks until there are nine blocks in a three-block by three-block setting.

Completed 3 x 3 block setting

When the green lines that outline the individual blocks are extended, they identify the larger grid for the Shadow layer. Our drawing now has two layers: one for small blocks and a larger grid for the Shadow.

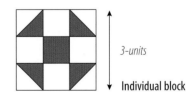

3-units

Individual block

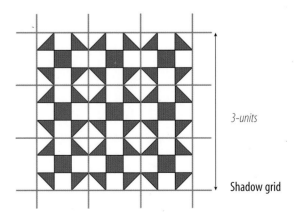

3-units

Shadow grid

Drawing the Shadow Layer

Fill in the negative space (background) of the individual blocks to create the Shadow.

Step 1. Refer to one of the original Shoo-Fly blocks. Look at the upper-left corner unit. It is two half-square triangles, a background triangle, and a Shoo-Fly triangle. The Shadow repeats this unit on its grid in the same location. Draw a line diagonally through the upper-left unit in the top row of the Shadow grid to create the two half-square triangles. The line extends through the negative space from corner to corner.

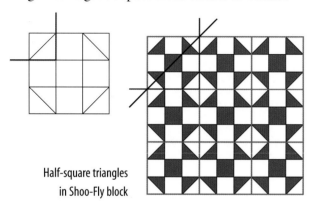

Half-square triangles
in Shoo-Fly block

Step 2. Use a third colored pencil to fill in all of the negative space of the individual block to create the Shoo-Fly triangle of the Shadow unit as shown. Do not color the individual block shapes that are already shaded blue. The red coloring creates a larger Shadow shape that duplicates the triangle in the individual blocks. The Shadow fills only the negative space. Do not re-color any of the original shading done in the individual block. Although the coloring for the Shadow appears to be incomplete when viewed up close, when seen from a distance, the eye fills in the blanks and the Shadow is complete.

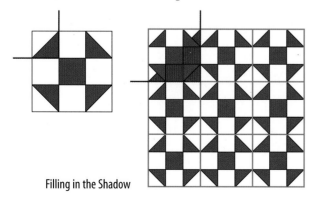

Filling in the Shadow

Step 3. Refer to the original Shoo-Fly blocks and continue duplicating the lines and shapes of the individual units on the Shadow grid. Each of the corner blocks has a triangle Shadow, and all of the negative space in the center block is filled in with Shadow coloring.

Completed Shadow layer

Can you see two layers? Does your drawing resemble the illustration? If you answered no, compare your design with the illustration, and analyze them both to see what needs to be corrected. If you said yes, congratulations, you've just designed a Shadow Quilt!

In essence, designing a Shadow Quilt is not difficult.

- For starters, keep it simple. Remember to establish the grid of your basic block and its Shadow.
- Create the individual block on its grid.
- Duplicate the individual blocks in each position of the Shadow grid. Create the Shadow in the background.
- Or begin with the Shadow layer first, and then place the smaller blocks on the grid.

If you are a newcomer to the design process, we encourage you to keep the designs simple at first for instant success. Even if you are an experienced designer, you might enjoy creating simple designs and using unusual fabric and color combinations. For your reference, potential blocks that meet the basic criteria are provided here.

Billie Mahorney used a fantastic combination of fabrics to create an exciting, original quilt from the Shoo-Fly drawn in this exercise. You can see her result "Shoo Fly From Outer Space" on page 20.

Blocks for Shadow Quilt Designs

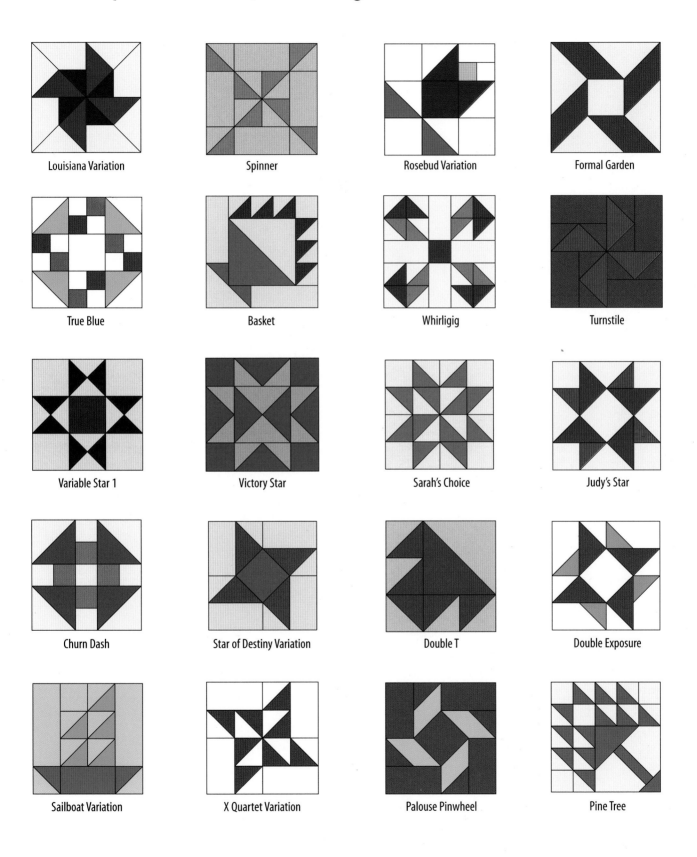

Louisiana Variation

Spinner

Rosebud Variation

Formal Garden

True Blue

Basket

Whirligig

Turnstile

Variable Star 1

Victory Star

Sarah's Choice

Judy's Star

Churn Dash

Star of Destiny Variation

Double T

Double Exposure

Sailboat Variation

X Quartet Variation

Palouse Pinwheel

Pine Tree

THE TRUTH IS ON THE INSIDE
Margaret Mustain de Leon
Arlington Heights, Illinois, 1999
61" x 61"

Primary hues and unusual fabric choices have turned this traditional Double X block into a striking overlay of color. The yellow dragonfly fabric echoes the original shape of the Double X block.

CHAPTER 3

From Our Stash

As quilt artists, our medium of choice is fabric. We prefer to use fabrics that are 100% cotton. We wash and dry them and put them away in our stash. When ready to use, the fabrics are ironed. Some quilters prefer to *not* pre-wash their fabrics because the sizing in the fabric helps keep the grainline stable. But each of us has had unfortunate experiences with colors running and fabrics shrinking when not pre-washed. We prefer to be cautious, but you should use any method that works well for you.

Designing a Shadow Quilt has been described as a playful, fun, agonizing, exciting, challenging, and freeing experience—all by the same person! These same expressions can also be used to portray the process of selecting a color scheme and fabrics that will bring the project to life. Once in a blue moon, everything will come together very quickly. Then there are the other times when it takes days or even weeks to finally settle on the just-right colors and fabrics.

Contrast

Being able to differentiate between the elements of the design is one of the most important considerations in any quilt, but is especially crucial in Shadow Quilts. Good contrast gives the Shadow and individual blocks their definition, and allows one of them to sing a solo while the other assumes the role of accompanist. If you try some "what ifs," beginning with value contrast, you will find that color and fabric preferences come together easier and faster. Three contrast categories contribute to successful combinations of colors and fabrics: value, temperature, and print designs. All interact with one another, and it is often hard to separate them when selecting color schemes and fabrics for a design.

Value Contrast—Light or Dark

After designing a project, we can't wait to begin the detective legwork that involves playing with colors and fabrics. We jump right into our fabric stash and try different combinations—beautiful floral prints, special plaids, wonderful small prints—trying to find the perfect grouping for this particular project. But in doing so, we skip over one of the most important steps in the process. A good way to begin any project is with value placement in the design.

Value is the lightness or darkness of a color. It refers to the relative amount of black or white that is combined with the color in a particular fabric. Use a mock-up to check fabric choices for value. Make a few blocks using the mock-up technique described on pages 57–61 if you are having doubts about value, or to be sure the fabrics and colors you are considering for a design will work. This simple process lets you double-check everything before diving into a project. It also has the advantage of using only small amounts of fabric.

The mock-up in the middle of page 26 depicts a value scale for the color blue. The center segment is the pure hue. As the eye moves to the left, the value of each fabric swatch becomes lighter with the addition of more white. Starting again at the middle of the scale and moving right, black has been added to create darker values. There are many degrees of value between very light and very dark within each color family. These swatches represent only a few of the many infinite gradations.

INTRIGUE
Eleanor M. Cole
Pullman, Washington, 1998
48" x 48"

The chevron design and a batik fabric that contained many of her favorite colors inspired Eleanor. The small blocks create a lattice that dances over the more subtle Shadow.

Value scale

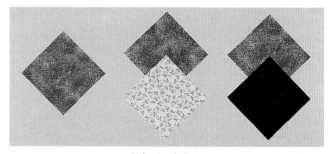

Value is relative

Value is relative. When we view a fabric, we can usually identify its value as light, medium, or dark. But place it next to a fabric with a different value and the value of our original fabric can suddenly change.

In the next column, the fabric on the left has a medium value, right? Sure, when it is by itself. But what happens when we put it next to a light fabric, as in the middle of the photograph? It appears darker. What happens when we put it next to a darker fabric as on the right? It seems lighter.

The value of any fabric is relative and can change, depending on the value of its neighbors. This impacts our fabric selection process. Don't select one fabric for your design without placing it next to the others under consideration to see if there is enough value difference. You need good value contrast between the background, the individual blocks, and the Shadow so each element will be perceptible. A value finder tool is very helpful at this point in the process. Hold this small piece of dark red acrylic up to your eyes and view your fabrics. The red takes out all the colors and leaves only value. If fabrics are going to blend together because of low contrast, you can see it now. If the fabrics can be seen separately and don't meld together, then they are a good, usable combination. A word of caution. Be careful when viewing red and green fabrics. The red value finder does not work well with its own color and its complement—green. Reds will appear unnaturally light and greens will appear much darker.

| Good value contrast | Poor value contrast |

The mock-up on the left depicts good contrast. There are enough differences in value between the background, the Shadow, and the individual blocks for one to be unique and recognizable. On the right, the fabrics for the individual blocks and the Shadow are too similar in value and moosh together. The result is not awful, but it is uninteresting.

Value contrast has many degrees of variation. High value contrast encompasses a wide range of values from very light to very dark. In this style, the quiltmaker uses fabrics from the far right to the far left of the value scale, from dark to light. Excitement and energy generally characterize these designs. Sharyn Cole created two quilts with high contrast: "I Want to See Stars" and "Now I See Stars" (page 29). Selecting values that do not have a very wide range on the value scale results in a scheme that has medium to low value contrast. To achieve this effect, eliminate the very lights and the very darks, and use only those values near the center of the value scale. Or take a grouping of values that are very near each other, but which don't venture too far to the left or right. The resulting definition of the design elements is more subtle and less sharp. Be careful. If the value contrast is too low, the Shadow and

individual blocks can meld and blend together. On the other hand, it can also produce a muted and softer effect. For example, Eleanor Cole's "Intrigue" has an overall feeling of richness and peacefulness.

High value and low value contrast can be combined to achieve a heightened effect. Note how Sharyn Cole used the blending effect in the outer blocks of "Now I see Stars" (page 29) by selecting fabrics very similar in value for the background and individual block elements. This created sharp contrast and allows the eye to focus on the Shadow and center of the design.

This table offers a few ideas for use of value in a design. You will probably discover other combinations.

Guidelines for Value

Background	Shadow	Individual Blocks	Example
Light	Medium	Dark	"Blue Plane Special" p. 35
Light	Dark	Medium	"Autumn Leaves: A Shadow Quilt" p. 96
Dark	Light	Medium	"Fire and Ice" p. 82
Dark	Medium	Light	"Winter's Night" p. 34
Medium	Light	Dark	"Cosmic Caper" p. 66
Medium	Dark	Light	"Intrigue" p. 26

| Medium individual blocks Dark Shadow, light background | Medium individual blocks Dark background, light Shadow |

It is interesting to see the visual effect of changing the values in a quilt plan. Let's try a "what if." We'll keep the values of the individual blocks constant in two mock-ups but play with the values of the Shadow and the background—reverse them for a different result.

Our eyes tell us that the same fabric was used in the two mock-ups on the right on page 27, but we find it hard to believe because they are so different. Changes in value placement make the difference. The individual blocks are made from a red fabric that is medium in value. These are the same in both designs. The dark fabric has been used as the Shadow on the left and the background on the right. The light background on the left becomes the Shadow on the right. Both are wonderful arrangements and would make beautiful quilts.

Temperature Contrast—Hot or Cold

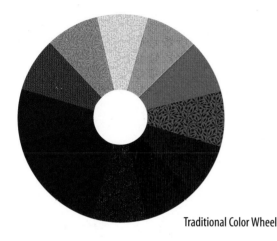

Traditional Color Wheel

Colors have either a warm or cool feel. The traditional color wheel, with its twelve segments, is positioned so yellow is at the top. All of the colors on the right side of the circle contain blue in various degrees. Blue, green, and some violets provide a sense of coolness, tranquility, freshness. The colors on the opposite side of the wheel contain differing amounts of red and transmit a feeling of warmth. Golden yellows, reds, oranges, and red-violets tend to be seen as energetic, active, and exciting. Warm hues tend to come forward in the design and are very eye-catching. A little bit goes a long way. On the other hand, cool colors recede and do not have the same strong impact as the warmer colors.

To see how temperature effects a design, let's play with some "what ifs." What happens if we have a cool or warm Shadow? Cool or warm individual blocks?

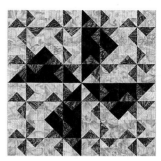

Cool Shadow
Warm individual blocks

Temperatures reversed

The example on the left has a cool Shadow and warm individual blocks. The one on the right has the temperatures reversed. Neither is better than the other; they are just different effects. When we examine these mock-ups in terms of value, we notice that both Shadows are dark. The one on the left has individual blocks that are relatively close to the Shadow in value. The red blocks on top of the Shadow are not lost because of the temperature contrast. In the example on the right, the individual blocks have a higher value contrast with the Shadow and are more visible. "My Little Neck of the Woods" (page 32) and "Road to the Sunset" (page 33) have both accomplished contrast through the use of a warm/cool combination.

Temperature contrast is valuable for distinguishing between elements. In the quilt "Celestial Encore" (page 47), Donna has chosen a palette of fabrics with very little value contrast. Most of the fabrics are medium value. Only a few lights are included and they are located near the center and in the twisted-ribbon border. The shadow is red (warm) and the individual blocks are green (cool). Because of temperature contrast, we are able to see each design element in the quilt.

Guidelines for Temperature

Individual Blocks	Shadow	Example
Warm	Cool	"Untitled 5" p. 11
Cool	Warm	"Jewel Box" p. 85

I WANT TO SEE STARS
Sharyn Floriani Cole
Redmond, Washington, 1998
24" x 24"

Sharyn used a lovely grouping of colors and fabrics to

create this interpretation of the Sawtooth Star block.

Bead embellishment gives a sparkle to the stars.

NOW I SEE STARS
Sharyn Floriani Cole
Redmond, Washington, 1998
16" x 16"

In her second version of the Sawtooth Star, Sharyn

has reversed the values and discovered it provided

more contrast. She much prefers this rendition to

the one pictured above. Beading and metallic

threads used for quilting add highlights.

TWILIGHT SHADOWS
Kiyomi Kalter
Apex, North Carolina, 1999
47" x 47"

Based on a traditional pinwheel design. After

making the light version of the quilt on page 31,

Kiyomi decided to see if the color transparency

effects would be enhanced on a dark background.

She likes this version best.

Warm and cool individual blocks
Warm Shadow

Again, these are only suggestions. As Donna played with drawings for this section, she also tried a combination of warm and cool individual blocks placed on a warm Shadow. The quiltmakers whose works are pictured throughout the book used a wide selection of temperature combinations to create a variety of effects.

Just for fun, let's try another "what if." What happens when we deliberately think about selecting placement of color and fabric using value and temperature together? Let's make two mock-ups and keep the background the same value and temperature (light cool) and reverse the temperatures and values of the Shadows and individual blocks.

Cool dark Shadow
Warm medium individual blocks

Cool dark individual blocks
Warm medium Shadow

We have another set of sketches to add to our growing collection. You will probably like one plan more than the other, but that's personal preference. Both designs are quite acceptable. We could continue on with the "what ifs." For example, what happens if we change the background from light to dark as Kiyomi Kalter has done in her "Twilight Shadows" and "Dawn Shadows" quilts. What if we switch the values and temperatures? See how one idea leads to another? Check out more

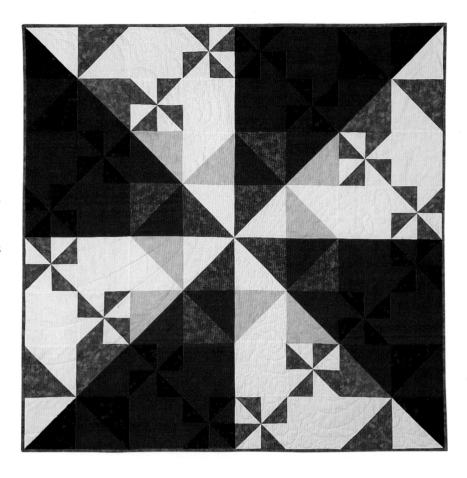

DAWN SHADOWS
Kiyomi Kalter
Apex, North Carolina, 1999
47" x 47"

Kiyomi used a traditional pinwheel design in several sizes and colors. The small pinwheels are set in opposite directions to create motion. Color changes have been used to give the effect of transparency.

options by examining the photographs of quilts throughout this book. Look for warm/cool combinations, then look for value placement. Study how the quiltmaker achieved that special effect with careful arrangement of values, temperature, and hues. Or who knows, maybe it wasn't planned at all, but was a serendipitous happening. We can always hope!

Print Design Contrast—Busy or Calm

Fabrics either have a solid look or are a print. Solids and the tone-on-tone prints that read as solids from a distance are calm in nature. On the other hand, prints that contain many colors and values look busy. To better understand the make-up of these different fabrics, let's do some surveillance to look at the specific characteristics that make them unique.

Print Design Elements

Before the fabric goes through the mill and the design is imprinted on it, a team of artists and graphic arts staff spend many hours perfecting this creation. The

following characteristics and guidelines help them produce a beautiful bolt of fabric that entices us to feel it, imagine how we would use it, and then buy it.

Contrast refers to variances in hue, value, intensity (bright or muted), color, and line; all combine to create the print seen on the surface of the fabric. If there is a wide range of differences, the high contrast results in a busy print. If the contrast is low, the print will appear almost as a solid.

Line describes the marks in the print design. Some lines are angular, straight, or hard. Look for these in plaids and stripes and geometric prints. Soft, curving lines, such as those found in florals, add grace and fluidity to the print.

Scale describes the size of the print on the surface of the fabric. Small prints tend to be calm while medium and larger designs appear busy.

MY LITTLE NECK OF THE WOODS
Terry Waldron
Anaheim Hills, California, 1998
Machine quilted by Pam Clarke
Spokane, Washington
56" x 64"

A traditional tree block becomes a medallion with a

summer Shadow. The smaller blocks depict various

stages of autumn. Terry's palette of unique fabrics

adds zing and brings the quilt to life.

Symmetry Does the print appear balanced and even, or lopsided and uneven? A symmetrical print appears very controlled and is methodically arranged. Calicoes, checks, ginghams, and some plaids and stripes are examples of fabrics that are symmetrical. These fabrics radiate tranquility. On the other hand, asymmetrical prints contain motifs that are offset and irregular. One has to look hard to find the repeat of the fabric. Paisleys, medium- and large-scale florals, representational prints, and fun juvenile designs all seem asymmetrical. They convey motion and action.

When we combine a palette of prints for a project, they must sing together as in a chorus. If there are too many soloists, we want to clamp our hands over our ears; too many busy prints in our design, and our eyes will ache. On the other hand, if the music is too serene and doesn't change its inflection, it becomes monotonous.

Guidelines for Print Design— Busy or Calm

	Busy	Calm
General over-all contrast	high contrast	low contrast
Value	wide range of values	narrow to medium range of values
Intensity	bright	muted
Lines	angular, sharp, whirls, geometrics, etc.	soft, graceful, slowly curving, etc.
Scale	large and medium	small and medium
Symmetry	asymmetrical	symmetrical

ROAD TO THE SUNSET
Nancy Larson-Powers
Pullman, Washington, 1999
49" x 49"

Nancy modified the Fly Foot block to create this exotic design. Africa was the inspiration for the color scheme. An elephant leaves the border and enters the quilt for a unique touch.

The mock-up below on the left uses busy prints in the background, the smaller blocks, and the Shadow. The effect is pretty chaotic, although it could have been worse! Substituting a calm fabric for any one or two of the elements would help bring order out of the chaos. The example below on the right shows what happens when only solid-seeming fabrics are used. The overall look is flat and uninteresting, lifeless and dull.

This mock-up has a nice balance of busy versus calm. Subtle prints that read as solid from a distance were selected for the background and the individual blocks. They nicely balance the busy Shadow print.

Good balance

So how do we mix busy and calm to come up with a suitable balance? An interesting palette has a variety of prints and solids, and uses them in such a way that they do not compete with each other or take over the design. If you want to have an active, exciting quilt, then use mainly busy prints. However, be sure to include enough calm pieces in your grouping to give the eye a place to rest. If you want the project to

Too busy

Too calm

WINTER'S NIGHT
Laurie Bevan
Woodinville, Washington, 1996
39" x 39"

These simple Friendship Stars light up a winter's

night. Laurie has selected fabrics that add sparkle.

The swirling and curving quilting lines provide a

nice contrast against the straight lines of the stars.

Owned by Debbie Vaught.

appear tranquil or serene, select fabrics that are relatively calm. Butremember to throw in a few pieces that have richer or brighter qualities to add accent, zing, and spice. Usually your own eye will tell you what looks good and what doesn't. We often hear the following comments in our classes: "Oh, that's too wild for me!" or "I think this piece needs to be jazzed up." Use your own good judgment to come up with an array of fabrics that pleases you.

Getting It All Together

There is no magic formula for choosing an assortment of fabrics. We both use a method that begins with too many choices. We go to our stash (or the quilt shop) and pick out a wide variety of prints in our color scheme that might work in this project. Then we begin to "subtract" the ones that don't work as well as others. It becomes a comparison test. Which is better, this busy print or that one? Should I substitute a calmer print? What about a plaid? A floral? and so on. We find that subtraction works better than addition. If we start with one or two fabrics and try to add additional fabrics one at a time, it becomes a difficult process for us. However, some people love to use the addition method. We would encourage you to use a style that works well for you. And when you are stumped, ask friends or people in the quilt shops. They all love to give free advice. Just remember this is your quilt and you have the final say.

Color Inspiration

One of the most-often-repeated phrases we hear from quilters is that they can't put colors together. Now just stop and think. You dress yourself every day, don't you? Do you put together outfits with colors that clash and cause every head to turn and eyes to stare at you

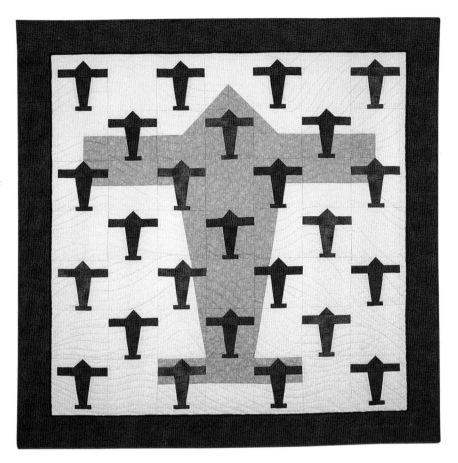

BLUE PLANE SPECIAL
Donna Ingram Slusser
Pullman, Washington, 1999
50" x 50"

Quilted wind currents are a backdrop for a squadron of
dark blue airplanes as they jet across the sky casting a
giant Shadow below. Alternate plain blocks add space
and keep the design from becoming too busy. Owned
by Sam Slusser.

as you walk down the street or step into the office? If
you can handle the task of color harmony in clothes (at
least most days), then you probably just need some
confidence and courage. Good detectives use their
imaginations to ferret out clues to solve their cases.
Let's adapt some of their techniques to find inspiration
for color schemes.

Confidence Builder #1

Go on a stakeout of Mother Nature. She puts wonderful color combinations together. In the spring,
discover how many shades of green decorate the land-
scape, from the light yellow-greens of new growth to
the deep, dark greens of the evergreen trees. In high
plateaus and desert regions, see how many variations
of tan there are and how different they look when the
sun is just coming up, at noon, and in the evening
shadows. Add some of those glorious lavenders and
red-violets and you have the basis for a beautiful

palette. Water is blue, right? Picture lights, mediums,
and darks, and then add a little green, or a little violet, and you have thousands of degrees of water hues.
Take a second look at the blooming rose. When it
first emerges from the bud, it is bright red with
lighter, coral highlights. As it becomes more full
blown, it gets darker, and finally turns the color of
wine. The leaves and stem provide a nice contrast,
warm against cool.

Confidence Builder #2

Gather evidence for a resource collection. We each
collect beautiful greeting cards and then never send
them, and buy gift wrap that never encloses a present.
They go in reference files for potential color schemes.
Filed with them are splashy or tranquil advertisements
ripped out of magazines. The mailbox is often stuffed
full of catalogs. Don't throw them away yet! First,
check out those dishes with the beautiful flowers

CHURNING OUT THE BLUES
Sharon Storment
Endicott, Washington, 1998
22" x 22"

Sharon used a wide range of blues to create a transparent effect. The soft tan Churn Dash Shadow gives a restful appearance.

painted on them, and that shirt with the lettering in that unusual combination of fuschia and olive-green. Cut them out and add them to the file.

And on it goes. Our file drawers are full and overflowing. Just seeing something before tucking it in a drawer seems to record it in our brain's data bank. Sometimes when we need a refresher course, we can browse through our files looking for that perfect combination of colors for the project we are planning.

We are also drawn to beautiful, colorful, or should we say, color-full books about art, decorating, gardening, and cooking. They are wonderful to peruse when relaxing with a cup of tea or a glass of lemonade. ("And chocolate," adds Patricia. "A nice gooey cinnamon roll," says Donna.)

Confidence Builder #3

Be a detective and shadow (follow) holidays, themes, and moods to see where they lead. Spring, summer, autumn, and winter each have a unique palette. Greens and reds bring a Christmas or December holiday to life; a Victorian look can be created by combining black with some florals and a splash of cream, pink, and a light green; try red and white for Valentine's Day. March 17 conjurs up great possibilities—as O'Slusser and O'Magaret, we dream of one day making an Irish theme quilt in green and white. Patriotism finds its expression in a variety of reds, whites, and blues. Country designs make wonderful use of muted colors. Contemporary jazzes things up while the reproduction prints lend an old-fashioned look. Plaids and stripes make us think of down-home comfort, a fire in the fireplace, and hot chocolate.

FIREWORKS
Betty Lee Swearingen
Tigard, Oregon, 1997
66" x 66"

The dark, cool Shadow provides a nice contrast for the smaller red blocks. The corners, which are composed of smaller twisted or "broken" pieces of the motif block, contribute to the symbolism of the exploding firecracker.

Quilts can have an emotional impact. Moods can be interpreted in colors. Are you blue today? Do you feel regal when working with violets and purples? What about friendly and warm? Or powerful, refreshing, serene? Let color express what you are feeling and what you want to convey to the viewer.

Confidence Builder #4

Invest in detect-a-quilt supplies. Do you collect certain types of fabrics although you don't know what you're going to do with them? Good. Keep adding to the stash and add new varieties and topics. Then, when you are ready to create a quilt, you will have the necessary ingredients on hand as Donna did when she and her daughter made "Pinwheels Spinning" (page 100). All the fabrics in this quilt were taken from her stash without any additional new fabrics. Patricia showcased fabrics from her batik collection in "Cosmic Caper" (page 66). Of course, both of us are now on a mission to visit quilt shops to replace the fabrics we used! Other fabric groups come to mind, such as ethnic designs, juvenile prints, musical themes, leaf fabrics, and so on. It's fun to find a fabric palette that gives your quilt a distinct personality. Collections of fabrics can be better appreciated in quilts than sitting on the shelf.

All sorts of fabric work well in a Shadow Quilt. Once you have your design, experiment with different types of fabrics, colors, values, prints, and solids. Make a mock-up if necessary. It will be a quick tool for helping you make fabric decisions. Try using them in the different elements of the design. See where they are most effective. Don't rush the process. The fabrics and colors you choose can either make or break your quilt design.

PEACE AND PLENTY
Carole Frye
Agoura Hills, California, 1999
49" x 49"

It is difficult to believe that this contemporary quilt is based on the

traditional Peace and Plenty block. The use of ombré fabric gives

light and dimension and sets off the center medallion.

CHAPTER 4

Spread Your Wings *and Fly*

Theme and Variations

In the world of music, a theme is defined as a group of notes that combine to make a melody that sets the tone for the composition. It is repeated several times during the course of the piece. Listen carefully and you will begin to recognize it when it reappears. Sometimes it is played as originally written; other times it has been changed to add variety and spice. The notes, rhythm, register (treble or bass), whether it is happy (major key) or sad (minor key), slow or fast, can all change in the variations. Some composers have written a multitude of variations on a single theme. They say it becomes a game to see how many modifications are possible. And so it is with Shadow Quilts. Now that you've learned the basic design technique (the theme), let's see how you can twist and turn the individual blocks, the Shadow, and even the background to make many variations.

Tools

In addition to the supplies and equipment mentioned on page 20, encourage yourself to use these devices.

Imagination

First, free your mind of any fences, walls, and mountains. Clear out the cobwebs and let your creative juices flow. Quilters are great problem solvers, and can come up with unique and fantastic solutions when presented with a challenge. Did you ever run out of a certain fabric when you are almost finished cutting out pieces for a project? Go to your stash and find something almost the same but not quite. Or come up with a plan for introducing a new fabric and scattering it among the others. Or if all else fails, go to your favorite quilt shop and cry, "Help!" Lots of free advice is always floating around. The point is, first let your dreams and ideas simmer on a back burner, and then let them boil over. Don't discard anything. Clarifying what you don't like is just as important as discovering what you do like. Explore and play with all of your ideas. One idea will often lead to another. And yes, we said play. It is really a lot of fun to try "what ifs." What happens if I take this out, put that in, move this here, move that over there, go outside the boundaries? Our imaginations—and playing with our ideas—are what led us on an adventure to discover some of the variations for Shadow Quilts. Best of all, we've come up with only a few of the endless possibilities.

Eraser

Remember to use both ends of the pencil. Using the eraser is almost like performing magic. What would happen if I took out this block, or this piece of a block? Erase it. If you like it, leave it. If you don't, shade or re-color the shape. Leaving out blocks and pieces of patterns is an important part of some of the variations.

Copy Machine

Copy! Copy! Copy! It saves time and energy. Copy a page full of drawn blocks, cut them apart, then arrange them on your quilt plan grid that has the Shadow in place. Try them in a symmetrical order, then in an asymmetrical arrangement. Rearrange those little blocks on the paper and explore all the possibilities. Just remember to stay away from open windows and fans!

Reference Page of Blocks

If you are stuck for ideas or need inspiration, there are blocks shown on page 23 that we think would make beautiful Shadow Quilts.

MYTERIES

We have uncovered six mysteries. These variations twist and turn the basic elements into something new. You will undoubtedly come up with more ideas as your creative juices start to flow. There are clues and ⊙━ keys to help conduct investigations into the way the blocks and Shadows have been arranged. They save you some legwork (or headwork) but you still need those sharp eyes and your best quilt deductive powers to solve the mysteries. Search for what is unique and different in each case, as well as what is similar, and see if you can solve the mystery before you come to our solution. The rewards are great!

Remember, these variations are just a few of the many innovations that can lead to new designs. Be sure to study the photographs of the quilts throughout the book. These quiltmakers all started with a simple Shoo-Fly basic block to learn this technique. Look where their journey took them!

Up to this point we have placed individual blocks in every position on the Shadow grid, as shown in this simple Shoo-Fly design. Thus, there are two layers.

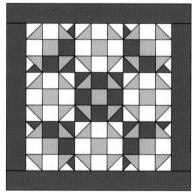

Blocks in
every position

Mystery—The Case of the Lost Shadow

⌀ This case has more than one solution.

After completing a design, we might decide that the quilt plan is too busy, or perhaps there is not enough negative space to make the Shadow easy to see. In this next illustration, notice how the design is chaotic; it is difficult to tell where the blocks end and the Shadow begins.

Chaotic design

Solution #1: Missing Blocks

⌀ **Alternate plain block setting**
Some individual blocks are missing in the following illustration. Notice that they disappeared in a very methodical order—every other block has been omitted.

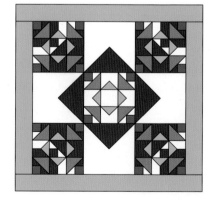

Design with
alternate plain blocks

⊙━ This quilt plan is known as the alternate plain block setting method. Pieced blocks are placed in every other position in the quilt plan and the remaining spaces are filled with non-pieced blocks. "Blue

Plane Special" (page 35) illustrates this perfectly. Traditionally, we would place pieced blocks in the four corners. The design might be equally interesting if the non-pieced blocks are placed in the untraditional locations. For example, when Patricia was playing with the previous illustration, she tried a "what if" and came up with this design.

Variation of alternate plain block design

This quilt plan works when the Shadow grid system is based on an odd number of equal divisions on each side, such as a 3-unit or 5-unit grid. Refer to page 14 for an explanation of grids.

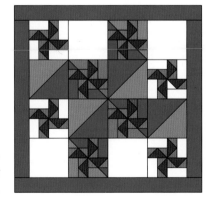

The design appears lopsided if an even-number grid system is used.

It seems like a simple solution to add an extra row of blocks to one side and the bottom. But now there is an odd-number grid system for the alternate plain blocks, and the Shadow is lopsided as shown. No matter where the Shadow is placed, the design will always have an unbalanced appearance unless it is offset.

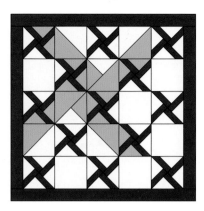

Lopsided Shadow

This part of the mystery cannot be completely solved right now. Use your quiltatronic surveillance equipment and watch for solutions in other variations.

Solution #2 : More Missing Blocks

Symmetrical exclusion of blocks other than alternate plain block setting

Individual blocks can vanish, but they needn't be every other-block as in variation #1. In this example, the plan remains symmetrical. "I Want to See Stars" (page 29) is a good example of omitting some of the blocks symmetrically. The designer of the following quilt plan decided to omit some of the blocks, but kept the arrangement of the remaining blocks symmetrical and orderly. This makes the Shadow more prominent in the design.

Symmetrical arrangement of individual blocks

Depending on the block and arrangement, you can use an even- or odd-number grid. See the following illustrations on page 42.

Even-number
unit grid

Odd-number
unit grid

Solution #3:
Help! More Blocks Vanish

Random exclusion of blocks

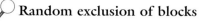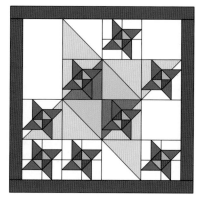

Small blocks vanish,
but this time they
didn't march off the
design page in an
orderly fashion.

 The designer randomly omitted the individual blocks. Notice how the asymmetrical placement of the blocks creates motion and excitement, and moves the

eye across the design. Test your surveillance skills to check out Patricia's "Phantom Fleet." This quilt would have been too cluttered if boats had been placed in all positions. We would have had to call out the Coast Guard for traffic control! Instead, the blocks are scattered as you might see them in the bay on a sunny and breezy day. Notice there are more boats near the bottom of the design than at the top. Placing visual weight below center is more pleasing to the eye than a top-heavy look.

Solution #4: Missing Pieces

Random fracturing of blocks

The blocks are
scattered across the
Shadow design.

Try using the eraser end of your pencil. Make some of those pieces vanish and see what happens. It opens up space and usually adds movement. Each block by itself doesn't look like much, but put them all together and you've got something unique. This variation can also help eliminate difficult piecing problems.

Notice that there are both whole stars and parts of stars in Becky Keck's quilt "Star Shadows" (page 44).

Mystery Solved!

Solutions #1, 2, 3, and 4 are excellent ways to solve the problem of a disappearing Shadow due to a busy setting or design and/or an overabundance of positive space in the individual blocks. But the case can't be closed—there are other payoffs waiting for creative detectives who can come up with even more variations.

PHANTOM FLEET
Patricia Maixner Magaret
Pullman, Washington, 1999
Machine quilted by Cheryl Swain
Genesee, Idaho
63" x 63"

Sailing along on a sea of blue and green, a phantom ship casts its shadow across the regatta as they catch the afternoon's breeze. Notice the asymmetrical placement of the small boats.

THE DOVE
Patricia Diaz
Lenore, Idaho, 1998
45" x 45"

The large Dove in the Window Shadow provides a backdrop for an asymmetrical assortment of smaller blocks. The theme is nicely carried out with a dove quilted in the center.

Mystery—The Case of "Which Way Did They Go?"

This case has several solutions.

Sometimes you may choose an asymmetrical block for the design.

That is, if you divided this pattern into four equal divisions, not all the divisions would be identical. The Basket block is a good example. Notice how it is tipped to one side. Rotate it a quarter of a turn and it tips to another direction. This tipping or directional look is characteristic of asymmetrical blocks.

A "tipped" asymmetrical block

Solution #1: The Blocks and Shadow Were Last Seen Together

Asymmetrical blocks and the Shadow all lean in the same direction.

When working with asymmetrical blocks, tilt them all the same way to create a directional effect. The viewer's eye follows the lines of the design from one side of the quilt to the other.

DIANA'S STAR
Jo Van Patten
Greenbank, Washington, 1998
33" x 33"

The traditional Road to Oklahoma block points a path to the future with a neutral Shadow and small blue blocks scattered over the surface. A smattering of beads and golden stars adds highlights that sparkle and twinkle.

GHOST BASKETS
Harriet Hosmer Watkins Mooney
Fox Island, Washington, 1998
60" x 60"

Use of the asymmetrical Basket block enabled Harriet to orient the Shadow in one direction while the individual blocks turn the opposite way. She felt the plain blocks appeared too solid, and used pieced baskets with a similar color and value to create the ghosts.

In Jo Van Patten's quilt, "Diana's Star" (page 45), she used the traditional asymmetrical block design, Road to Oklahoma. All the individual blocks point in the same direction as the Shadow.

Solution #2: Blocks and Shadow Have Split Up and Are Headed in Opposite Directions

Blocks lean in opposite direction

 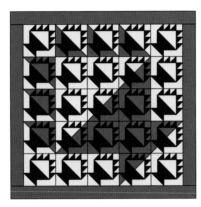

When using asymmetrical blocks, it is fun to design the quilt so the lines of the blocks and Shadow go in opposite directions. This time the viewer's eye will move first one way and then back in the other direction. There is a feeling of movement and balance.

In "Ghost Baskets" (page 45), Harriet Mooney chose to have the individual basket blocks lean in the opposite direction of the large Shadow basket. The overall effect is one of harmony.

Mystery Solved!

These two solutions allow opportunities to play with the tension between the individual blocks and the Shadow when using asymmetrical blocks. But we can't close this case yet—your quiltatronic surveillance methods can probably come up with more wonderful solutions to this case.

Mystery— The Case of the Line-Up

There are at least two solutions to this case.

Up to this point, we included a large Shadow on one layer, and smaller, individual blocks on another layer. The small blocks were all the same size. Let's try a "what if." What would happen if we were to reduce and/or enlarge some of those individual blocks?

Solution #1: Lots of Look-a-Likes!

Multiply the blocks

The units on the Shadow grid can be broken down into even smaller units to create more small blocks. In the illustration below, let's check out the upper-left corner unit in the individual block. It is blank. We would normally place one individual pinwheel block in that unit. What if we place four smaller pinwheel blocks in this unit and all the other units in this design? Wow! Lots of pinwheels. This means more piecing, but the effort might well be worth it. Donna liked this effect and used it creatively in "Celestial Encore."

 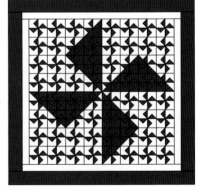

Effective use of smaller, individual blocks

Solution #2: Different Sizes for the Line-up

Use different sizes of blocks to create a multi-layer effect

What happens to the design if we place an individual block on one Shadow unit grid, and break down another grid unit to create smaller blocks?

CELESTIAL ENCORE
Donna Ingram Slusser
Pullman, Washington, 1994
39" x 39"

The Shadow in this Variable Star pattern is more pronounced than the individual blocks because of its warm color in addition to its size. The twisted ribbon border introduces luminosity and dimension.

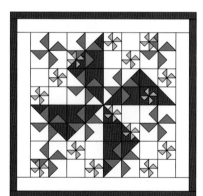

Three-layer grid

In this illustration, some of the units on the Shadow grid contain the "normal" one pinwheel per unit. Other Shadow grid units have been broken down and left empty, while others are filled with smaller pinwheels. This creates three layers—small blocks, medium blocks, and the large Shadow. Inspect Judy Imler's quilt "Seahorse Cotillion"(page 48). Note how she has enlarged some elements and reduced others in the Brown Goose block and then scattered them randomly across the quilt. She has created an exciting, exuberant design by utilizing scale variety, and gives a successful illusion of more than two layers.

The multi-layer concept can be enhanced by using softer, more solid, and more subtle fabrics in the most distant layer. Gradually work to flashy, eye-catching, more high-contrast fabrics in the topmost layer. "Cosmic Caper" by Patricia (page 66) illustrates this concept. The large gold Shadow star is similar in value to the background—not much contrast. The medium turquoise stars are darker but still contain the same color as the background, offering a little more contrast but not a lot. The small magenta stars pop off the surface as if they are coming toward us. These stars contrast with all the other elements in the design.

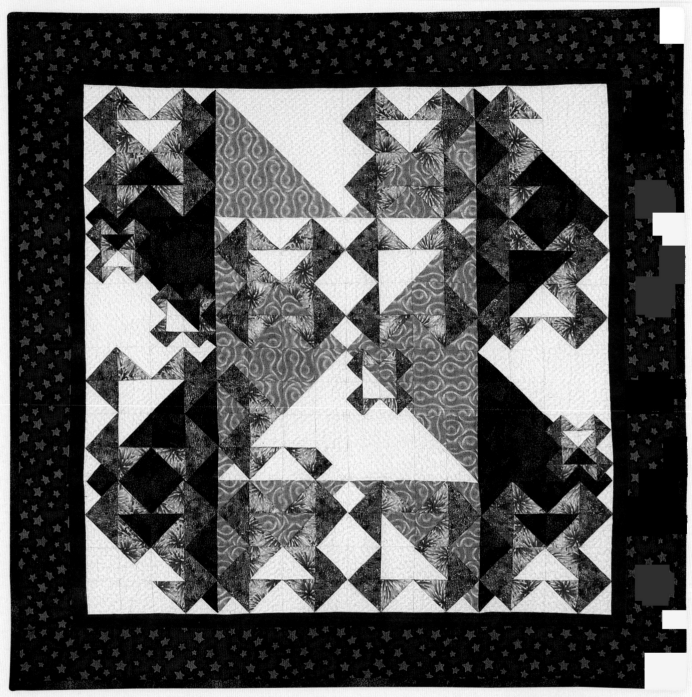

SEAHORSE COTILLION
Judith Ann (Furry) Imler
Colfax, Washington, 1998
Machine quilted by Rayanna DeFord
Colfax, Washington
45" x 45"

Judy used the Brown Goose block pattern. Parts of the design elements are missing, making your eye move across the quilt to fill in the spaces and find the seahorses.

Mystery Solved!

What fun to play with different block sizes and create new layers! But again, we won't close this case. Your shadowing and stakeout skills are probably giving you ideas for more big payoffs.

Mystery—The Case of the Rebellious Blocks

How many solutions can you find for this case?

So far, we have concentrated on placing the individual blocks exactly in the center of each unit on the Shadow grid. This is the most predictable and easiest type of Shadow quilt to design.

Individual blocks placed in the center of each unit

Let's try some "what ifs." What happens if the individual blocks are offset so they are no longer centered on the units of the Shadow grid?

Solution #1: Renegade Blocks

Offset Blocks

Some of the small blocks are rebels and refuse to sit in their places on the traditional Shadow grid. If they move as they wish in this variation and travel off-center, we can take advantage of more unusual design effects. "Escargot's Escapade" (page 50) effectively lets the Snail's Trail block creep out of the design, even beyond the border.

Blocks offset from Shadow grid

Some of the blocks could even extend into the border as shown in the next sketch. Notice that the corners of some of the individual blocks are sharing space with their neighbors for an intriguing effect.

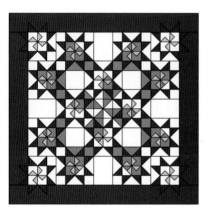

Blocks "escaping" into the border

The blocks in the next illustration present an even more radical departure from the Shadow grid and have pushed out even further into the border. This effectively opens up the Shadow and makes it more visible than in the previous example.

Blocks extend further into border

ESCARGOT'S ESCAPADE
Linda Bennington Devereaux
Lakewood, Washington, 1999
39" x 39"

Richly textured fabrics wend their way across the quilt in a Snail's Trail design. Some of the blocks extend out of the quilt to create visual excitement and interest.

Solution #2:
Mixing Up Odds and Evens

Perhaps we want to open up the Shadow even more by adding space to the outside of the conventional Shadow grid.

Space added to the
Shadow grid

An even-unit block can now be placed on an odd-unit Shadow grid system. In this case we added a half-block of space to all four sides of the Shadow grid, creating a five-unit grid for a four-unit block. Now the Shadow is the center of the design.

Reforming Rebel Blocks

Designing these variations may be a little more difficult. The first illustration on page 51 shows what to avoid. Notice how the renegade blocks have plunked themselves down wherever they wish. There are not many common lines to facilitate easy block construction. In this scenario, piecing could become a nightmare.

Work (and play!) to find common lines between the various elements in the design. First, draw the Shadow on graph paper. For the next step, you need multiple individual blocks to play with. Either draw them on graph paper or use a copy machine. When finished, cut out these blocks and move them around on the Shadow drawing, placing them where you see common lines between the small blocks and the Shadow.

ECHOES OF WINTER
Doris Northcutt
Greenbank, Washington, 1999
35" x 43"

Winter is depicted by an unusual combination of

colors and fabric textures. The overlap and variation

in tree size contributes to the dimensional look.

This makes piecing less tedious. Also, common lines help unify the design. In the illustration below, the designer was attracted to the circular effect of the blocks over the Shadow. However, the top, bottom, and side blocks are out of sync. Look what happens in the illustration at right when they are each moved just a little. The illusion of circular motion is still present, piecing is simplified, and the look is more harmonious.

A simplified design
means easier piecing

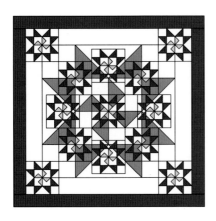

Rebellious blocks
could create piecing
nightmares

O━━ The design process is easier when you use a drawing program on your computer. Draw your Shadow on one layer. Draw the individual blocks on the next layer up. Again, move the blocks around, taking care to find common lines between the layers. You can quickly discover many pleasing variations. What would we do without high tech?

WHIRLIGIG AWHIRL
Patricia Maixner Magaret
Pullman, Washington, 1998
Machine quilted by Cheryl Swain
Genesee, Idaho
44" x 44"

This simple Windmill block comes to life with

an unusual combination of colors and fabrics.

The pieced border repeats the pinwheel motif

found in the center of each block and nicely

frames the quilt.

Doris Northcutt's quilt "Echoes of Winter" (page 51) illustrates a design that has blocks offset from the Shadow grid.

Mystery Solved!

Being a rebel means taking some risks. Pushing the boundaries of the traditional Shadow Quilt plan grid will create some interesting and exciting designs. Is this case closed? Nope. We hope your undercover work has your imagination working overtime on how to work with those rebel blocks. Hopefully you've been sketching ideas in your little notebook while doing surveillance. We can see another big payoff coming!

Mystery—The Case of the See-Through Shadow

There are at least two solutions for this case.

We have been discussing multi-layer designs in which the individual blocks appear to sit on top of the Shadow. It appears this way because parts of the Shadow are hidden behind the block elements. How can we make the Shadow appear to be sitting on top of the blocks?

Solution #1:
Looking Through the Shadow

Transparency Effect

It appears we can see through the Shadow.

 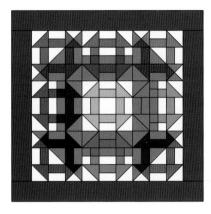

Transparent effect

To achieve the illusion of looking through the Shadow, you will need to add extra lines. The Shadow lines extend through the block units.

 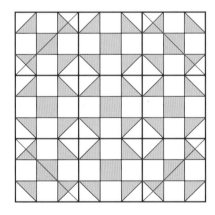

Adding extra lines through blocks

Fabric selection is the key to the success of a transparent design. Wherever there is a crossover, there is a color change. There are two ways to accomplish the illusion of transparency.

Method 1: Where the Shadow covers the blocks, select a darker value of the block color. It also helps if these two fabrics have similar prints. Sometimes you can even find the same print in different colorways. In the Shoo-Fly pattern in the next illustration, notice that when the block units are covered by the Shadow they are a darker red. It gives the illusion of looking through a blue film.

In her quilt "Whirligig Awhirl" Patricia was able to find two colorways of the same print. She used the lighter one in the background. The darker print became the Shadow. It appears as if a tan film is sitting on top of the windmills and outer border.

Using light and dark to create transparency

Method 2: Where the Shadow covers the blocks, imagine what color would result from mixing the two colors together. A color wheel (page 28) is a good tool to help make this determination. For example, red mixed with blue makes violet; blue mixed with yellow equals green; red combined with yellow creates orange. In the illustration below, note that where the blue filmy shadow covers part of the red blocks, the Shadow turns to a dark violet.

 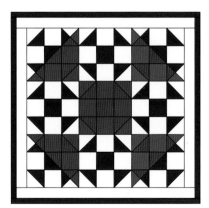

Mixing colors to achieve transparency

This second method sounds easier to accomplish than it actually is. It might be a good idea to make a mock-up first to be sure that your fabrics will create this effect.

TULIPS ABOUND
Ginny Mayer
Clinton, Washington, 1998
45" x 45"

Like a breath of fresh air, these tulips are
breaking forth in spring splendor. Ginny used a
yellow tulip overlay for the Shadow that creates
the illusion of transparency.

Notice the transparency in Ginny Mayer's quilt, "Tulips Abound." Where the large sheer tulip covers the blocks below, there is a color change.

Mystery Solved!

The illusion of transparency can be difficult, but well worth the challenge. A good detective will see through the shadows to create a Shadow Quilt that seems tailor-made for this special effect. But as always, the case remains open! Your shadowing techniques will lead you to more solutions!

Mystery—The Case of the Wanted Poster

How many variations or solutions can you find?

Up until now we have used one block for the individual blocks and the Shadow. What happens if some of the members of the rebel group change appearance? Perhaps the Shadow is disguised so it no longer resembles the individual blocks. Maybe the individual blocks all decided to change their appearance so they no longer resemble one another as much as they did when they were clones. Yet they still remain members of the troupe.

Solution #1: The Leader Is Disguised

 The Shadow is a different block pattern

Mixing block patterns

 This design uses a Windmill block for the Shadow and a Shoo-Fly pattern for the individual blocks.

The Shadow layer and the individual blocks can be related by theme as in these two blocks.

Another example is the design (above right) that features Anna's Basket Shadow (an original block by Patricia) with Tulip blocks scattered across it. What a lovely springtime theme idea.

The sky is the limit. A word of caution: When combining several patterns, use blocks that have common lines to aid piecing.

In Donna and Patricia's quilt, "Sew This Is What Quilting Is All About" (page 68), a sewing machine is used for the Shadow. Quilting equipment motifs and simple blocks make up the smaller blocks. This design was computer generated using a drawing program. The Shadow was developed on the first layer and all the motifs were drawn on a second layer. These were then moved around until common lines were found with the Shadow and the overall design was visually pleasing.

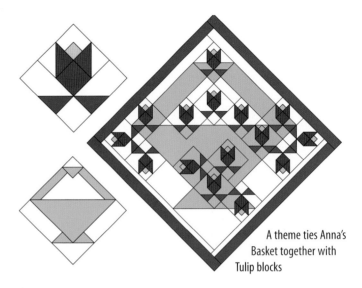

A theme ties Anna's Basket together with Tulip blocks

Mystery Solved!

Talk about blocks disguising themselves but still wanting to be related! Thank goodness there is a theme to help us identify what is happening in this exciting variation. We can't close this case yet. Ideas are coming too fast! Big rewards are ahead!

Good Detectives

We have only touched the tip of the iceberg when discussing the design potential of Shadow Quilts. Every day we have new ideas that we want to try and it seems that every day has six hours too few. Our students have given us new ideas as a result of their questions and curiosity. By asking "what if?" we have all learned to experiment. It has been rewarding for us to see beginning quiltmakers design a simple Shadow Quilt, then push on to variations of their original theme. The more they play with their ideas, the faster the possibilities bubble up to the surface. Soon designing goes beyond Shadow Quilts. Masterpieces are the result. It is like a child coloring in a coloring book—at first the pictures are very exact, perfect, and pretty. But imagine what might happen if this budding artist starts to color outside the lines. You never know unless you try.

SHADOW PINWHEEL
Myrna Teade
Colfax, Washington, 1998
20" x 20"

A beautifully framed mock-up, this design was inspired by the colors in the busy background

fabric. Myrna wisely kept the blues and teals used in the Shadow and individual blocks rather

calm. A light narrow inner border floats on the background and adds a nice accent.

CHAPTER 5

Mock-Up Magic

Do you wish you were a good detective—a terrific "tail"—who could "follow that car" to the most wonderful fabric shops to find the most perfect fabric? Quilters have been known to agonize over fabric selection and color schemes for hours, days, weeks, and — dare we say it out loud—even months! Wouldn't it be wonderful to use a technique that lets you audition ideas quickly? And when finished have a product worthy of framing? Mock-ups are perfect to use for the audition process, and they seem almost magical when Steam-A-Seam 2® or another adhesive is used.

A framed mock-up is a beautiful, thoughtful gift, even to yourself. Myrna Teade was thrilled with the final result of her mock-up "Shadow Pinwheel." It is often missing from the walls of her home because it is displayed at her local quilt shop where it brings many "oohs and aahs." Susie Borowicz's mock-up, "Second Growth Forest" (page 59), is an original design based on a tree block. Marilyn Ahnemiller made a large mock-up (not pictured) of her bed-size ribbon quilt (page 58). She made the mock-up before cutting into the fabrics to check fabric and value placement. In *From Our Stash* (page 25), Patricia made the color wheel mock-up, and Donna's husband, Lloyd, made the pinwheel designs. Borders have not been added to these mock-ups, yet they are suitable for framing.

Our first experience with mock-ups was a long, arduous process. We made only two of them as class samples because of the difficulty we encountered when we used glue sticks and adhesive spray to attach teeny-weeny fabric pieces to posterboard, and coincidentally to nearby tables, chairs, walls, floors, and various body parts. Then we discovered that using Steam-A-Seam 2 made the process truly magical and easy.

It is not necessary to make a full mock-up; a few blocks might be enough to check fabrics, colors, and value placement. Once you see that everything works together, then you are off to cut into the fabric to make a traditional quilted project.

So let's begin the auditioning process. A few simple supplies will get you going.

Supplies

Backing Materials
We have used both posterboard and foam-core board. The foam core requires an Exacto® knife or razor for cutting. If you are concerned about deterioration over time, use an acid-free mat board found at art supply and frame shops.

Adhesive
We prefer to use Steam-A-Seam 2. However, other products will work, including glue sticks and spray adhesive. Steam-A-Seam 2 is a double-stick, iron-on fabric fusing web. It is applied to the back side of the fabric and then you can cut the two together into the desired shapes. Because it is a double-stick webbing, it adheres to the fabric before the fusing process. It can be repositioned until it is permanently bonded.

Rotary Cutter and Mat
Use for accurate cutting of pieces.

Rulers
6" x 24" ruler for marking the grid

6" x 12" ruler for cutting fabric

1" x 6" ruler for cutting fabric

TIE A YELLOW RIBBON
Marilyn Lorinne Ahnemiller
Hoodsport, Washington, 1999
95" x 95"

Marilyn made a mock-up of this colorful quilt to be

sure that the colors and values of the fabrics would

produce the effects she wanted to achieve. The

shaded golds and yellows of the Shadow nicely

wrap up the quilt.

Make a Mock-Up

Determine Grid Size

How large should the mock-up be? We make ours in the 20"–30" range. They can be made any size by following these steps. Instructions are for a square mock-up. If you use other shapes, make the necessary adjustments. Grid size is usually based on 1", 1½", or 2" squares. The grid size does not include borders.

Step 1. Count the number of individual units on one side of a block. Multiply this number by the number of blocks per side. For example, the pinwheel designs in Chapter 3 have four units per side for each individual block. There are four blocks per side in the design.

4 units x 4 blocks = 16 units on each side of the design

Step 2. Multiply the total units per side number by 1", 1½", and 2" for three different size options. For

other sizes, use the inch (or partial inch) increment that gives the desired size. In our pinwheel example we have the following options:

16 x 1" = 16" x 16" grid before borders

16 x 1½" = 24" x 24" grid before borders

16 x 2" = 32" x 32" grid before borders

Mark the Grid

To check for accuracy:

Mark only a small portion of the grid. Apply Steam-A-Seam 2 to the back side of a small piece of fabric. Cut only a few pieces and apply to the grid. Inspect closely to see if everything fits nicely. Now is the time to make necessary adjustments for marking the grid or cutting the pieces if necessary.

SECOND GROWTH FOREST
Susan Borowicz
Elk City, Idaho, 1998
32" x 32"

Susan made this mock-up for her club's yearly

challenge with the theme, "Our Heritage."

Framed and hanging on the wall in her home,

this design adds a nice touch to her décor.

Use a sharp pencil and accurate ruler to mark lines. To be very precise, we first estimate the completed size of the grid, mark the grid increments on all four outside edges, then connect the lines.

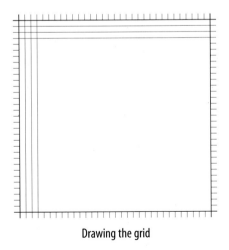

Drawing the grid

Apply Steam-A-Seam 2

Step 1. Determine the approximate amount of yardage needed for each fabric.

Step 2. Apply Steam-A-Seam 2 to the back side of the fabric according to manufacturer's directions. Do not remove the second sheet of paper at this time.

Step 3. Use a rotary cutter and ruler to cut the shapes needed for the design. Be accurate. Remember there is no ¼" seam allowance.

Position Fabric Shapes on Grid

Step 1. Peel paper from the fusible webbing. If the paper is difficult to remove, a straight pin can help lift it off, starting at a corner.

Step 2. Place fabric shapes on the grid. To give the design a smooth appearance, apply all of the background pieces first, then add the other fabrics.

PURPLE PASSIONS
Cathy Erickson
Washougal, Washington, 1999
60" x 72"

Peony blocks twist and turn to encircle their Shadow in
this beautiful quilt. Sprays of ribbonwork flowers bloom
in opposite corners. The watercolor-type border adds a
subtle but definite frame.

HOT SUMMER DAY AT DONNA'S
Sharon Hyslop Wiser
Pullman, Washington, 1998
19" x 19"

Sharon hand-dyed the fabrics for this quilt at her group's annual summer party "dyeing on Donna's patio." The color run from yellow to turquoise contains an exciting mix of both muted and bright colors.

Donna first makes one traditional block without the Shadow fabric, then makes a second block with the Shadow. These two blocks will show whether fabrics, colors, and value placement will work together to accomplish her goals. If she doesn't like how things look, she carefully lifts the shapes off the background, often using the point of a seam ripper to get a corner started. She then carefully repositions the pieces until she finds a satisfactory arrangement.

Finishing

If desired, add borders to the mock-up.

When the project is completed, permanently adhere the fabric to the backing by following the manufacturer's directions on the Steam-A-Seam 2. We place the backing on a flat surface, fabric side up. Position a slightly damp towel over the surface. Press with a medium-hot iron, leaving it in one position for only a few seconds. After the pieces are dry, we check to see if a second steaming is needed for the shapes to adhere securely to the backing.

Frame the finished mock-up. Give it to a lucky friend or relative or be nice to yourself and say, "This one's for me!"

Mock-ups can also be used for other projects. Make individual blocks of the Variable Star or Drunkard's Path quilt you want to make. Audition different fabric and color schemes until you find the perfect combination. You can make a single block or finish the mock-up to create a small piece. Frame and enjoy!

KIMONO KEEPSAKE
Donna Ingram Slusser
Pullman, Washington, 1997
72" x 72"

Dipping into her collection of Asian fabrics, Donna took the basic T-block

pattern and turned it on point so it resembled kimonos. Quilting with variegated

rayon thread highlights the soft blue Shadow Kimono and adds texture.

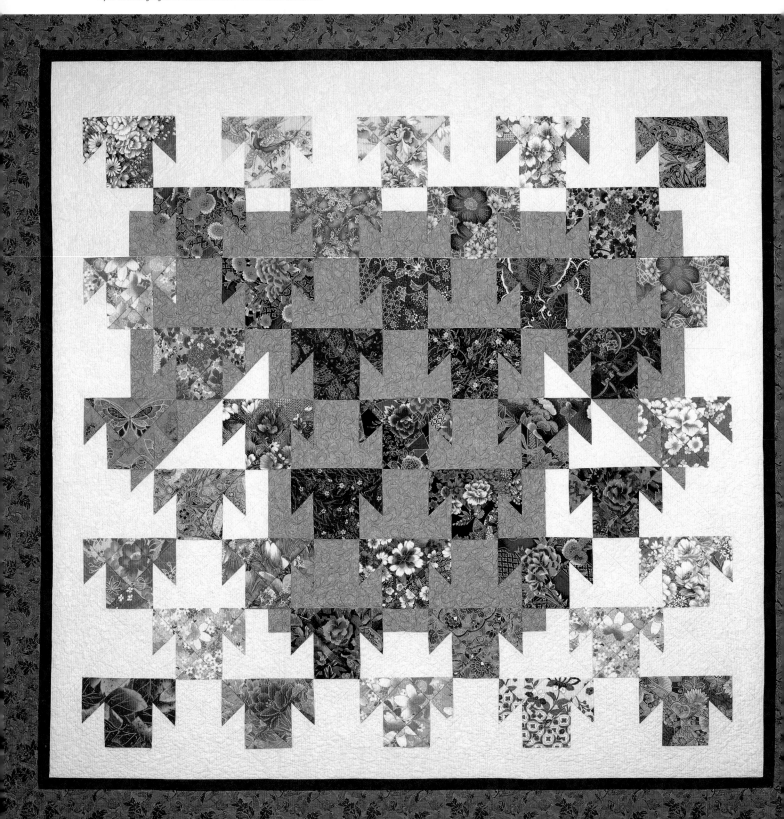

CHAPTER 6

High-Tech Design

When we started quilting in the early 1980s, we had to learn a new language: quilt-speak. We also made our own templates out of stiff paper and then drew around them on fabric. We hand-cut the pieces using scissors, one layer at a time. Talk about time consuming! Then along came the rotary cutter and mat. Remember how scary it was to hold that pizza-cutter-type tool in one hand while your other arm applied pressure to the long ruler? Ah, but it took a lot of the laborious work out of the quiltmaking process, and now these tools are part of our daily lives. Here we are again, in the midst of another revolution—the computer age. Scary thought, but not so bad once you try it—just like rotary cutters.

We both became part of the high-tech generation when Patricia's son Craig encouraged her to get Internet access and take advantage of e-mail. Soon Donna was "wired" too. Prior to this momentous revolution, we had mainly used our computers for word processing and spreadsheets. The step-up to the Internet gave us the confidence we needed to explore other uses for the big boxes with screens that sit on our desks.

Patricia had always used graph paper for designing quilts and tracing paper to create layers of designs on top of other designs. Donna finds graph paper frustrating and almost more trouble than it is worth. She does admit, however, that it is essential to use it for Shadow Quilt designing. Because she is a visualizer, Donna is able to go to the design wall and arrange different fabric patches to create unique patterns. Patricia is more visually challenged, but should own stock in a graph paper company.

We both experienced a breakthrough from computer paralysis, and were delighted when we found software programs for drawing and quilt design. For us, graph paper is going the way of the dinosaur. We have found that we can create quilt designs quickly, then generate variations at the speed of lightening. It works for us. Patricia used a draw program to design "Cosmic Caper" (page 66) while Donna used a quilt program to create "Kimono Keepsake."

Computer design is not for everyone. You need to decide if you can be comfortable in front of the screen, holding a mouse in your hand. Are you ready to invest in software that will get you off graph paper and into twenty-first-century design? It takes time to master the new tools that are at your fingertips. Be patient. If you are persistent, there are all kinds of rewards.

We are not going to elaborate on computers or specific software programs and how they work. We are quilters, not engineers. The high-tech field is changing so rapidly that by the time you read this, any specific information we give will be obsolete. Instead, we will talk briefly about the various types of software available and give a thumbnail sketch of how we use our programs. Again, our information is not intended to be complete because of the shelf life of the current versions.

Now when we have an idea, we go to our computers and quickly sketch a plan. We then rotate and move blocks, "tweak" things a bit, and then audition colors. It all seems so magical. The two quilt plans on page 67 are from Patricia's file (and pile!) of drawings she executed electronically.

Quilt Design Software

Quilt software was designed specifically for quiltmakers. There are several programs on the market, and we suggest that you find a way to test-drive each of them before making a decision about which is best for your needs. These programs are simple enough for beginners, yet powerful enough for the more experienced quilter.

In these programs you can choose from libraries of block designs or create your own blocks. You can put color and fabric texture where you want in the blocks and place them into a quilt format. Borders and sashing can be automatically added or omitted. These programs also print blocks, quilt designs, and templates in varied sizes. They also calculate yardage. Because they were designed for the quilter, they include valuable hints and tips to make quiltmaking easier and more efficient. You can get technical support by phone, mail, or e-mail. This is very helpful for those of us who quiver at the keyboard. Several programs also offer foundation-piecing options, with a library of blocks that can be printed in various sizes and used immediately.

Quilt design software does have drawbacks. However, again, by the time you read this, new features may have been added and these insufficiencies corrected. The drawing tools included are limited, and block manipulation and transformation is restricted. Most quilt programs will not allow you to work in layers, although there are some shortcuts to get around this. However, as a general statement, they are capable of accomplishing the tasks that most quilters need. They are user-friendly and the prices are very reasonable.

Donna uses a quilt design program regularly, and finds it an invaluable tool for creating quilt designs, handouts, blocks for classes, and foundation-piecing designs. At present, her program does not have the capacity to create multi-level designs, although an updated version looks promising. To make the present program work, Donna uses the following guidelines.

Step 1. Determine the number of different drawings and shadings for the blocks of the design. Let's use our

investigative skills. Look at the pattern for "Jewel Box," beginning on page 85. How many different blocks are needed to make the design? Answer: three. Yes, only three.

Block 1 Basic individual block: one shading

Blocks 2 and 3 The basic individual block with a diagonal line drawn from corner to corner: two shadings

Step 2. Draw these blocks and color or shade them. In our "Jewel Box" example, there is one shading for four individual blocks, one shading for eight blocks that contain the red portion of the Shadow, and another shading for four blocks that have the purple shading for the Shadow.

Step 3. Place the blocks in their correct location in the quilt plan and rotate each one as needed to achieve the correct orientation.

Step 4. Audition other colors. Play with value and warm/cool contrast. Add borders and print!

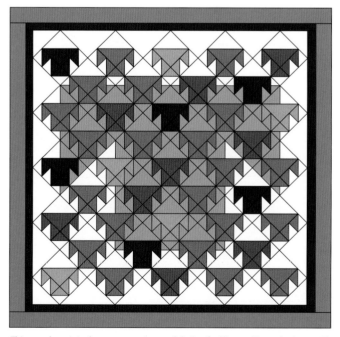

This was the original computer-generated design for Kimono Keepsake (page 62). Donna used quilt software to determine whether the simple T-block could be used effectively as a Shadow Quilt. She drew the six different blocks, then placed them in the design.

Drawing Software

Drawing software allows the designer more capabilities and flexibility, and more tools are available for sophisticated drawing. You will be working on a gridded computer screen that resembles graph paper. These programs are vector-mapped—in other words, lines are drawn on a pathway of points. When lines enclose an area, that area becomes a shape. Each shape or patch can be drawn, colored, and textured, if you want them to look like fabric. The options for texturing are usually very limited. The shapes can be grouped to make a block, and blocks duplicated and moved around on the screen. They can be overlapped, stretched, distorted, and manipulated in a number of ways.

The layers feature is particularly valuable when designing Shadow Quilts.

Step 1. Draw the background Shadow block on the first layer.

Step 2. Go to Layer Two and draw small blocks. They will be opaque (unless you have and choose to use a Transparency option). Even though you are working on a new layer, you will be able to see the Shadow on Layer One. Move the small blocks around until you are pleased with the overall effect. Look for common lines between the Shadow and the small blocks to make piecing as easy as possible.

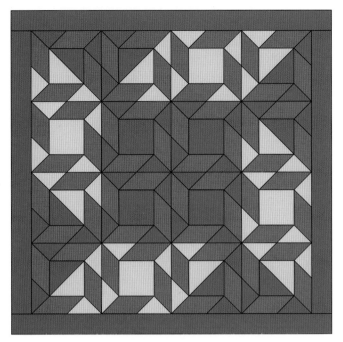

Completed design with Shadow and blocks layers

For more fun see what happens if you add another layer. Remember that the highest numbered layer will be the blocks that are resting on top of your design and closest to you.

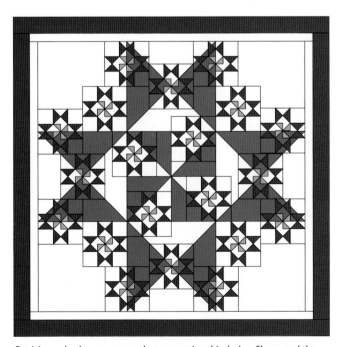

Patricia used a draw program when generating this design. She moved the individual blocks across the Shadow until the over-all effect was pleasing. Piecing lines can be added or cleaned up later.

COSMIC CAPER
Patricia Maixner Magaret
Pullman, Washington, 1999
Machine quilted by Cheryl Swain
Genesee, Idaho
56" x 56"

The batik background fabric sets the tone for the colors in this three-layer design. The warm/cool contrast of the stars on each layer adds tension and excitement.

Drawing programs are not designed exclusively for quiltmakers. They do not have pre-loaded libraries of block designs or fabric textures. You have to use your imagination. You can't calculate yardage or print templates. Also, the price tag on some of the high-end drawing programs will elicit a big "Gulp!"

Individual blocks have been moved off-grid and some were omitted

Some quiltmakers feel that drawing programs are not as user friendly as the quilt software. You might want to try experimenting with them first. Many of the software companies have websites where you can download a trial version. This gives you the opportunity to see if you like the program before you open your wallet. Phone and e-mail technical support is also available to answer questions and solve your problems.

Which software to use? It depends on what you want to do with it. Patricia draws the illustrations for our books and for all of her class handouts on a drawing program. She prefers the freedom, versatility, and power of this software. Donna uses a quilt design program because she can produce quilt designs with fabric texture. She also likes the feature that conveniently

prints quilt blocks at any size with accurate seam allowances and templates that are conveniently numbered. Check out some of our projects designed with the aid of our computers: "My Cup of Tea" (page 12), "Mantilla for Mom" (page 16), "Blue Plane Special" (page 35), "Sew This Is What Quilting Is All About" (page 68), and "Passing Through" (page 104).

Once you become familiar with either a quilt design program or a drawing program, you will find that computer-generated designing is a lot of fun. That's the bottom line. Your eyes will be opened to a new world, just waiting to be explored. Experimenting with a mouse and a computer screen and hitting the print button is much faster and less expensive than experimenting with fabric. Good luck, high-tech friend.

A rectangular design with individual blocks placed in a circular pattern

SEW THIS IS WHAT QUILTING IS ALL ABOUT
Patricia Maixner Magaret and Donna Ingram Slusser
Pullman, Washington, 1999
51" x 51"

The Shadow sewing machine with its appliquéd heart symbolizes

the passion of all quiltmakers. Sewing motifs are scattered over the

quilt and were embellished for dimensional effects.

CHAPTER 7

General Project Guidelines

Accurate Piecing

Use an accurate ¼" inch seam allowance when making templates, cutting, and piecing. Even the smallest mistakes can quickly compound a problem.

Fabric Requirements

We have calculated amounts of fabric needed for the projects based on 42"-wide, 100% cotton fabric. A small amount of additional fabric, approximately 4"–6", has been added for security and errors (heaven forbid!), or, if you're lucky, adding to your stash. You may need more or less fabric, depending on how you cut pieces and which method you use. If your fabric is not 42" wide, you'll need to adjust the amounts. Fabric requirements for binding are measured for a ½"-wide finished binding. Make the necessary adjustments if you prefer a different width.

Fabric Grain

Threads that run parallel to the selvage are called the lengthwise grain. They are very stable and have little stretch. Threads that run from selvage to selvage are known as crosswise grain. Fabric is also stable on the crosswise grain, although there is some give or stretch. Both lengthwise and crosswise threads are straight-of-grain. True bias is a 45° angle from the lengthwise and crosswise grains. Bias also refers to any cut that is not on the straight-of-grain. The fabric stretches very easily on the bias.

Grain line is important, particularly when cutting strips for borders and binding. Generally speaking, cutting on the lengthwise grain is best for borders because of the lack of stretch. Binding needs some give so bias or crosswise grain are most commonly used.

Straight-of-grain lines are marked on templates and pattern pieces. Follow these lines so no bias cut is on the outside edge of a block or quilt top.

Pressing

First and most important, pressing is not ironing. It is the lifting up of the iron and placing it back down on the fabric, rather than pressing with a back-and-forth motion. There are varied opinions about whether or not to use steam, and whether to finger press or use the iron. Because steam can cause shrinkage and distortion, we both prefer to use a dry iron until the quilt top is finished. We then give the top a good steam press on both the front and back sides. We both prefer using an iron rather than finger pressing during unit and block construction. (Wow—we agreed on a subject!)

We also prefer to press seams to one side, preferably toward the darker fabrics when possible. Some quilters elect to press their seams open to cut down on bulk. We like to set the stitches before pressing the units, blocks, and borders. Here's what we do:

Step 1. Place the piece(s) to be pressed on the ironing surface, wrong side up. Pressing on the wrong side prevents the tucks and pleats that can occur when pressing from the front side. It also helps to avoid the shiny appearance that often results from over-pressing.

Step 2. Press the iron for a few short seconds on a portion of the seam allowance or surface to be pressed.

Step 3. Lift the iron and move it to the next location on the seam allowance. Press.

Repeat until the entire seam allowance or surface has been pressed.

No-Template Method for Cutting Triangles

There are many methods for cutting and piecing half-square and quarter-square triangles. Use the technique that is most comfortable and accurate for you. We recommend the following technique.

Half-Square Triangles

Step 1. Determine the finished size of the square. Add ⅞". Cut a square to this measurement.

Step 2. Cut the square in half diagonally. Yield: two half-square triangles.

Important Note: The straight-of-grain is on the shortest sides of the triangle, usually the outside edges of the unit or block.

For example, for a 2" finished square use this formula:

2" + ⅞" = 2⅞"

Cut a 2⅞" square, then cut in half diagonally.

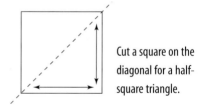
Cut a square on the diagonal for a half-square triangle.

Quarter-Square Triangles

Step 1. Determine the finished size of the square. Add 1¼" to this figure. Cut a square to this measurement.

Step 2. Cut the square in half diagonally twice. Yield: four quarter-square triangles.

Important Note: The straight-of-grain is on the longest side of the triangle, usually the outside edge of the unit or block.

For example, for a 2" finished square use this formula:

2" + 1¼" = 3¼"

Cut a 3¼" square, then cut in half diagonally, twice.

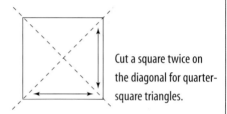
Cut a square twice on the diagonal for quarter-square triangles.

Borders

We prefer to cut border strips on the lengthwise grain, even though it requires more fabric. The fabric requirements for each project quilt allows for cutting the borders on the lengthwise grain. Lengthwise grain has little or no stretch, making it very stable. Trim the selvages first and then cut strips parallel to the outside edge. Use the remaining fabric for block pieces and for adding to your stash.

Measuring for the Length of the Border Strips

No matter how careful we are, finished quilt tops often have edges that have been stretched because of handling and pressing.

Sometimes the extra length is minimal while other times it may be several extra inches. If border strips are cut to a length using an outside edge measurement they may ruffle and the quilt will not lie flat.

To avoid this problem, measure through the **center** of the quilt: top to bottom for side border strips, and side to side for top and bottom border strips.

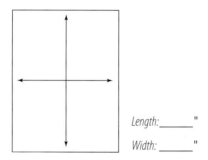
Length:_____"
Width: _____"

Our projects allow extra length for the border strips. They need to be trimmed to the proper length. Cut border strips to the measured length on the lengthwise grain.

Adding Borders to the Quilt Top

Whether to use straight-set corners or mitered corners is a matter of personal preference for quilt-makers. Both of us usually favor mitered corners for our projects, although you will find straight-set corners on some of our quilts pictured in this book. Mitered corners are a little more difficult and take a little more time, but are well worth the effort.

Straight-Set Corners
Attach the side borders first, then add the top and bottom border strips.

Step 1. Measure top to bottom through the center of the quilt top to determine the length measurement for the border strips for the two sides of the quilt top. Cut or trim strips to this length measurement. Mark centers and quarter points with pins as shown.

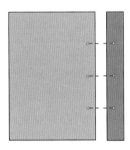

Step 2. Mark quilt top side edges at the center and quarter points with pins as shown.

Step 3. With right sides together, match marker pins of the border and quilt top. Pin together, easing fullness as necessary. Sew borders to the sides of the quilt top. Press seam allowances toward the borders.

Step 4. Measure side to side, including borders, through the center of the quilt top to determine the measurement for the top and bottom border strips. Cut or trim strips to length measurement. Mark centers and quarter points with pins as shown in Step 1.

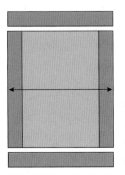

Measure across the center of the quilt to determine the top and bottom borders.

Step 5. Mark the top and bottom edges of the quilt top at center and quarter points with pins as shown in Step 1.

Step 6. Match marker pins of border and quilt top as shown in Step 1. Pin together, easing fullness as necessary. Sew borders to the top and bottom of the quilt top. Press seam allowances toward the borders.

Mitered Corners

The project instructions allow extra length for the border strips so they can be trimmed to the correct length before joining to the quilt top. When there are two or more borders for a project, sew all the border strips together for one side, then repeat for the three remaining sides. Add each of the side units to the quilt top as if they were just one border.

Step 1. Measure through the center of the quilt to determine the width and length of the quilt top.

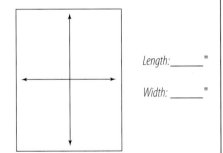

Length: _____"

Width: _____"

Step 2. Determine the width of the borders and **double** this figure.

For example, if the width of the border is 4", 4" x 2 = 8".

Step 3. Add the doubled border width to the width and length fig-

ures in Step 1. **Add an additional 4" for security.** Cut two border strips this length.

For example,
width: 30" + 8" + 4" = 42" cut length for two border strips

length: 45" + 8" + 4" = 57" cut length for two border strips

Step 4. Fold each border strip in half to find the center and mark with a pin. On the top and bottom border strips, measure half the width measurement determined in Step 1, going away from the center mark in each direction. Mark with pins.

For the two side border strips, similarly measure half the length measurement determined in Step 1. Mark with pins. Measure to determine quarter points and again mark with pins. There will be a few extra inches on the ends of all the border strips; this is used for the mitering.

Step 5. Find the center and quarter points of each side of the quilt top and mark with pins.

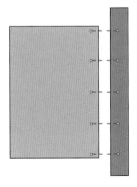

Step 6. With right sides together, pin borders to quilt top, matching pin markers and easing fullness as

necessary. Stitch, using a ¼"-wide seam allowance. Begin and end stitching ¼" in from each corner of the quilt top. Backtack. Press seam allowances toward the borders.

Step 7. To miter the corners, place one corner on the ironing board, right side up. Pin if necessary to keep the quilt flat and secure.

Step 8. Fold one of the borders under at a 45° angle. Work to create a perfect angle and to make sure that the edges meet correctly. Double check with a square ruler. When everything is accurate, lightly press with a dry iron. This fold line is the sewing line for the mitered corner.

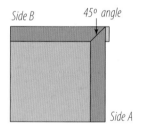

Side B   45° angle
Side A

Step 9. Carefully turn the border of Side A up to match the edge of Side B. The quilt is now folded on the diagonal with the wrong side exposed. Pin across the fold line to secure.

Step 10. Beginning at the outside edge of the border strip, stitch on the fold line. Stitching stops ¼" away from the inside edge of border. Backtack at beginning and end of stitching.

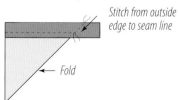

Stitch from outside edge to seam line

Fold

Step 11. Trim the seam allowance to ¼" and press open. Repeat for all corners.

Quilting

The basic guideline for creating a quilting pattern for a Shadow Quilt is to use lines that enhance the overall beauty of the design. Keep lines simple to match the character and nature of the quilt. These quilts are probably not the place to use feathers and other fancy motifs. Such figures compete with the design for our attention, and they can detract from the impact of what has been depicted.

In general, we recommend quilting in the ditch around the main elements of the design. Use an over-all quilting pattern in the background and sometimes over the Shadow. Examples of over-all stitching lines include stippling, meandering, cross-hatching, curving lines, rays, wind currents, and so on.

Patricia is a hand quilter, but is trying to learn how to quilt with her machine. So far her success is limited, but she is practicing, practicing, practicing. When hand quilting, Patricia uses 100% cotton thread. She uses many thread colors to obtain the effect she wants. Her philosophy: You can never have too much quilting.

When quilting a Shadow Quilt, Patricia emphasizes the components of the individual blocks by stitching in the ditch to make them stand out. For example, when using a star pattern, she would

stitch around each star point. She then chooses two close over-all patterns—one for the Shadow and another for the background. The differences in texture between the background and Shadow add interest. The closeness of the stitches makes these areas lie flat so the individual blocks pop forward.

Donna begins thinking about quilting designs of a project about halfway through the sewing part of the quilt. She finds herself starting to ponder these questions: "I wonder what kind of quilting lines will bring these fabrics and colors to life? What do I want to emphasize in this design—the Shadow or the individual blocks? What type of stitching should I do in the background?" Sometimes she doesn't know the answers to all of these questions when she begins to quilt. Donna is a machine quilter, which means that the first quilting stitches will be in the ditch around the outside edge of each block to help secure the layers together and to create manageable sections for further, more elaborate quilting. She uses Harriet Hargrave's method described in the book, *Heirloom Machine Quilting*. After completing this task, Donna usually has the answers to her questions and is ready to begin the stitching lines that are unique to this quilt.

In most of her Shadow Quilts, Donna next outlines (stitch in the ditch) the individual pieces in each block, and then fills in the Shadow and background.

Sometimes the Shadow and background are treated as one large area with one quilting design, as in "Autumn Accents" (page 8). Notice that each triangle and square in the individual blocks were outlined. Then gentle curving lines suggesting wind currents were stitched in the background and over the Shadow. A variegated rayon thread that blended with both the background and Shadow fabrics was used in the top needle. A neutral colored, 100% cotton thread that blended with the top thread was used in the bobbin. In other quilts, Donna uses different stitches in the Shadow and the background. In "Kimono Keepsake" (page 62), after outlining each block, the individual kimonos were quilted using straight lines with variegated rayon thread in the top needle and a neutral colored, 100% cotton in the bobbin. The Shadow fabric appeared rather flat and dull, so a more detailed quilting pattern was used to bring it to life. The same threads were used as before. The background area of the design contains a random, meandering stitch, similar to stippling except some lines cross over others. These curving lines add texture to this part of the quilt and are a nice counterpoint to the straight lines of the kimonos. An off-white, 100% cotton thread was used in both the top needle and the bobbin.

Binding

When the quilting is finished, remove all basting and pins. Use a rotary cutter and ruler to trim the quilted sandwich layers so they are even. Be sure the batting lines up with the raw edges of the backing and quilt top so it will fill the binding. Square the corners with a square acrylic ruler.

Fabric Grain

Consider the grain of the fabric when cutting strips for binding. Bias has a lot of stretch. Many quilters, including Patricia and Donna, prefer this type of binding. If the quilt has curved or scalloped edges, the binding must be cut on the bias. Crossgrain cuts also yield fabric strips with some stretch. Fabric strips cut on the lengthwise grain have little or no stretch. The type of binding you use is a personal choice.

Double-Fold Binding

A double-fold binding is a lengthwise strip of fabric that has been folded in half, and provides a strong, good-looking wrapped edge for the quilt.

Binding Length

Figure the length of binding needed for the project.

Step 1. Add the measurements of the four sides.

Step 2. Add an extra 20" for turning corners and security.

For example, if your quilt measures 30" wide x 45" long:

$$30" + 30" + 45" + 45" = 150" + 20" = 170"$$
Length of binding = 170"

Binding Width

The width of the binding is a matter of personal taste. Most bindings are ¼"-½" wide when finished. We both prefer narrow bindings, usually ¼" finished. To calculate the width of the strips needed for a double-fold binding, cut strips six times the finished width of the binding plus ¼" (a little extra to allow for the turn of the cloth). For example, if you want a ½" finished binding, cut the strips 3¼" wide.

$$½" x 6 + ¼" = 3¼"$$

Making the Binding

There are several methods to use when preparing the binding. Donna prefers to cut bias strips and sew them together for binding, while Patricia cuts continuous bias binding from a square of fabric.

Cutting Strips

Cut strips on the lengthwise or crosswise grain; for bias binding, cut strips on the 45° diagonal. For all types of binding, sew the strips together using diagonal seams (see diagram). Trim the seams to ¼", and press them open. Press the strip in half lengthwise, wrong sides together.

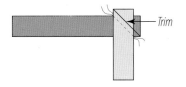

Continuous Bias Binding

A fast method to use when making bias binding is to sew and cut the fabric strips in one continuous operation from a single square of fabric.

Step 1. Determine the size of the square needed as follows.

Multiply the length of binding needed by the cut width of the bias strip.

Length of Binding x Cut Width of Bias Strip = X

Use a calculator to find the square root of X.

Round this number up to the nearest inch and cut a fabric square of this size.

For example, a quilt that measures 30" x 45" requires 170" of binding.

The desired binding is ¼" when finished so strips are cut 1¾" wide.

170" x 1¾" = 297.5

The square root of 297.5 is 17.25. Cut an 18" square of fabric.

Step 2. Pin mark the top and bottom edges as shown. Draw a diagonal line as shown and cut on this line.

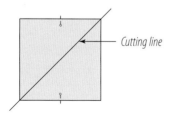

Cutting line

Step 3. Match the pins, and sew the two triangles right sides

together, as shown below. Press the seam open.

Step 4. Line up a ruler parallel with bias edge A. Make a cut 3" in length at the desired width of the bias strips (in our example, 1¾").

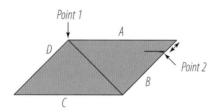

Point 1

A

D

Point 2

B

C

Step 5. Bring the right sides of non-bias edges B and D together to make a tube of fabric. Align the edges and match points 1 and 2. Pin edges together. Stitch using a ¼" seam allowance and press the seam open. The tube now has a 3" tail at one end and an extension on the other end.

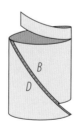

B

D

Step 6. Place a small rotary-cutting mat on an ironing board and place the tube around the end of the ironing board. Be careful not to stretch the tube. Cut a continuous-bias strip at the desired width as illustrated. Press the

continuous-bias strip in half lengthwise, wrong sides together.

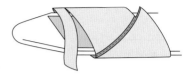

Applying the Binding

Step 1. Fold the beginning of the binding strip at a 45° angle. Press toward the raw edge of the binding.

Step 2. Beginning near a corner of the quilt, place the binding strip on the front side of the quilt, right sides together, aligning the raw edges of the binding with the raw edges of the quilt. Stitch the binding to the quilt. The stitching line makes a seam allowance that is as wide as the finished width of the binding. For example, for a ¼"-wide finished binding, stitch the binding to the quilt using a ¼" seam allowance. Be careful not to stretch the binding or the quilt top when stitching.

Step 3. When nearing a corner, stop the stitching line exactly the width of the seam allowance from the corner. For example, if the seam allowance is ¼", the stitching line will stop ¼" from the edge. Backstitch, clip the threads, and remove the quilt from under the presser foot. Turn the quilt.

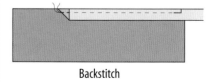

Backstitch

Step 4. Fold the binding straight up and away to form a 45° angle fold.

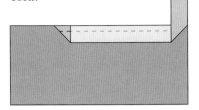

Step 5. Holding the diagonal fold in place with a finger, bring the binding straight down on top of itself. The raw edges of the binding should align evenly with the edge of the quilt. Begin stitching at the top of the fold in the binding. Backtack to secure, and continue stitching until you reach the next corner, when the process is repeated.

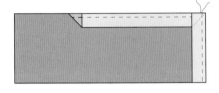

Step 6. Continue stitching around the quilt, mitering all corners. When you near the starting point, overlap the beginning binding strip 1" beyond the beginning stitches. Backtack and clip threads.

Step 7. To finish, turn the binding over the raw edges to the back side of the quilt. Blindstitch the folded edge of the binding just through the backing layer. Be sure the stitches do not show on the front.

Step 8. To miter the binding at the corners, stitch up to a corner. Fold the miter on the back in the opposite direction from the miter on the front side of the quilt. Secure miters with several stitches on front and back. Continue stitching until the binding is completely fastened.

Hanging Sleeve

If your quilt is to be displayed on a wall, it needs a sleeve for a hanging rod at the top of the backing.

Step 1. To make a 4" finished (finished size) pocket, measure the top edge of the quilt. Cut a strip this length by 8½" wide. To hem the short ends, turn under ½" and press. Turn under ½" again, press, and stitch in place.

Step 2. Fold the sleeve in half lengthwise, right side out. Pin and sew the length of the sleeve ¼" from the raw edges.

Step 3. Place the tube on a flat surface with the seam centered on one side. Press the seam open.

Step 4. Center the sleeve so the raw seam allowances are next to the quilt backing. Pin to the top edge of the back of the quilt ½" below the binding. Hand stitch all four sides to the back of the quilt, catching some of the batting in the stitches. Be careful that the stitches do not go through to the front of the quilt.

Step 5. Place a rod or length of pre-measured lath (purchased from a building supply store) in the sleeve. Hang your quilt and enjoy!

Labels

Several years ago, Patricia had a devastating experience. One of her quilts was stolen. She did not have her name on that quilt, so now it is "anonymous." That bothers her more than anything. So she now steps up on her soapbox and encourages quilters to make sure they don't make the same mistake.

No quilting project is completed until it is signed and/or labeled. We are all artists, and artists always sign their work. We recommend that you sign on the quilt top, when first completed. Later if you wish, you can also make a fancy label to appliqué onto the back of your quilt. We suggest that you use a permanent fabric marking pen on the front. Feel free to use any permanent pen or handwork on your back label.

The information to include on every quilt is:

Your complete name.
Date the quilt was completed.
Location where the quilt was made.

Any other information you include will be valuable to your family, friends, and quilt historians in the future.

For fun and future interest, transfer a photo of the quiltmaker onto the fabric and include that in your label.

The more information we include about ourselves, as quiltmakers today, the more valuable our quilts will be as the history of tomorrow.

Shoo Fly
Don't Bother Me

Patricia Maixner Magaret
Donna Ingram Slusser

Pullman, Washington, 1999
Quilt Size: 43" x 43"
Block Size: 9" finished

The simple Shoo Fly block is given a new look in this Shadow quilt.

The border design was added by Billie Mahorney in her quilt on

page 20. This version uses warm individual blocks and a subtle floral

print for the Shadow with cool borders to create visual contrast.

Shoo Fly Don't Bother Me

Do you recognize this design? It is based on the simple Shoo Fly block we used in Designing a Shadow Quilt (page 17) and is an excellent example of how a simple block can be used to create a design that appears complicated. The border design is based on the one Billie Mahorney chose for her quilt on page 20. Different borders would give this project an entirely new look. For example, one simple wide border would provide a nice frame around the blocks.

FABRIC REQUIREMENTS

42"-wide fabric. A few extra inches have been included for security, correcting mistakes, and for adding to your stash.

Background/Pieced Border
Light: ¾ yd.

Individual Blocks
Red: ½ yard

Shadow
Tan Floral: ½ yd.

Inner Border*
Lavendar: ⅞ yd.

Pieced border
Green: ⅓ yd.

Outer Border and Binding*
Dark Green: 1½ yds.

Backing 1½ yds.

Batting 47" x 47"

* Fabric amount allows for cutting border strips on the lengthwise grain and for ½"-wide bias binding. Cutting borders on the lengthwise grain will help your quilt lie flat. See page 70 in *General Project Guidelines*.

Fabric Tips

This project uses a warm/cool combination to create contrast between the center design and the borders. A light background fabric with warm undertones sets the stage for design. A calm tone-on-tone red print is used for the individual blocks that sit on top of the tan floral print of the Shadow. The triangle border is a medium green while a darker green makes up the outermost border. The combination provides a nice frame. The lavender narrow inner border is a contrasting color and effectively encloses and sets off the center design.

Our palette is rather muted. Brighter jewel-tone colors, plaids, or florals would give different effects to suit your décor.

Cutting

Refer to page 70 for cutting half- and quarter-square triangles.

Background (Light)
Cut twenty-four 3½" squares.

Cut ten 3⅞" squares, then cut in half diagonally.

Cut two 4¼" squares, then cut in half diagonally twice.

Individual Blocks (Red)
Cut nine 3½" squares.

Cut eighteen 3⅞" squares, then cut in half diagonally.

Shadow (Tan Floral)
Cut twelve 3½" squares.

Cut four 3⅞" squares, then cut in half diagonally.

Cut two 4¼" squares, then cut in half diagonally twice.

Borders

All border strips include a few extra inches for length variations. Strips will be cut to the correct length before you sew them to the quilt top.

First Inner Border (Lavendar)
Cut four strips on the lengthwise grain 1½" x 32".

Outer Border (Dark Green)
Cut four strips on the lengthwise grain 4¼" x 45".

Pieced Border

(Light)

Cut seven 5⅜" squares, then cut in half diagonally twice.

(Green)

Cut eight 5⅜" squares, then cut in half diagonally twice.

Block Assembly

Block A: Make four blocks.

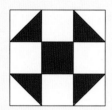

Step 1. Join four light triangles to four red triangles (cut from 3⅞" squares) as shown. Press.

Step 2. Join units and squares as shown. Press.

Block B: Make four blocks.

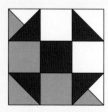

Step 1. Join a light triangle and a tan floral triangle to two red triangles (all cut from 3⅞" squares) as shown for Block A. Press.

Step 2. Join two tan floral triangles to two light triangles (cut from 4¼" squares) as shown. Press.

Step 3. Join these units to two red triangles (cut from 3⅞" squares) as shown. Press.

Step 4. Join units and squares together as shown. Press.

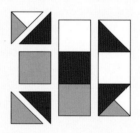

Block C: Make one block.

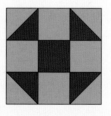

Substituting tan floral pieces for light pieces, construct as for Block A.

Quilt Top Assembly

Arrange blocks as shown in the quilt photograph. Sew blocks together in vertical columns, press. Sew the columns together, press.

Adding Borders

Inner Border (Lavendar)

Measure and cut the final lengths for the 1½" x 32" precut border strips following the information for mitered corners on pages 71–72. Sew to the quilt top using mitered corners. Press.

Pieced Border

Step 1. Sew together into strips: seven light and eight green triangles (cut from 5⅜" squares) as shown. Press. Make 4 strips.

Step 2. Sew border strips to quilt top using mitered corners. Follow directions on page 71–72.

Outer Border (Dark Green)

Measure and cut the final lengths for the 4¼" x 45" precut border strips following information for mitered corners on pages 71–72. Sew to the quilt top using mitered corners. Press.

Quilting and Binding

Layer the backing, batting, and top; baste. Stitch-in-the-ditch around the Shoo Fly and pieced border elements. Choose an overall background design for the remainder of the quilt. Refer to pages 73–75 for binding information. Attach a hanging sleeve or pocket to the top on the back side of the quilt. Finish by adding your label.

Shadow Play

Marie (Toodie) Blichfeldt

Vashon Island, Washington, 1998
Quilt Size: 39" x 39"
Block Size: 8" finished

Toodie interpreted the Louisiana block pattern in a warm/cool palette. The narrow inner border of background fabric adds open space and suspends the pinwheels.

Shadow Play

Toodie's design contains only two different blocks and uses simple shapes. A warm/cool combination of fabrics accentuates the design elements. Using two values of blue and two values of rust helps separate the Shadow from the individual blocks in the viewer's eye. The design appears to float because the inner border is the same fabric as the background. This quilt could easily become the medallion center of a full-size quilt by adding borders or enlarging the block size.

Fabric Tips

Keep the busy/calm aspect of fabrics in mind for this quilt plan. Because there is so much motion and activity in the design, Toodie wisely chose fabrics that are calm in nature. The cool blues found in the individual blocks contrast nicely with the warm Shadow. Be sure there is enough value contrast between all the fabrics so the individual blocks can be easily distinguished from the Shadow.

Audition different theme fabrics for a variety of effects. Plaids and stripes would give a homespun look. (Caution: Use those that are mainly small scale and calm.) Check out the array of beautiful batiks for a contemporary look. Create a nostalgic feel with the reproduction prints. Let your imagination fly!

Cutting

Refer to page 70 for cutting half- and quarter-triangles.

All border strips include a few extra inches for length variations. Strips will be cut to the correct length before sewing to quilt top.

Background (Light Tan)
First cut four strips on the lengthwise grain for the inner border 1" x 38".

Cut thirty-two 2½" x 4½" rectangles.

Individual Blocks and Border
(Dark Blue)
First cut four strips on the length-wise grain for the outer border 3½" x 43".

Cut sixty-four 2⅞" squares, then cut in half diagonally.

(Light Blue)
Cut sixty-four 2⅞" squares, then cut in half diagonally.

Shadow
(Light Orange)
Cut eight 2½" x 4½" rectangles.

Cut eight 2½" squares.

Cut eight 2⅞" squares, then cut in half diagonally.

(Medium Orange)
Cut eight 2½" x 4½" rectangles.

Cut eight 2½" squares.

Cut eight 2⅞" squares, then cut in half diagonally.

FABRIC REQUIREMENTS

42"-wide fabric. A few extra inches have been included for security, correcting mistakes, and for adding to your stash.

Background/Inner Border
Light tan: 1¼ yds. (includes allowance for inner border)

Individual Pinwheels, Outer Border, and Binding*
Dark blue: 1½ yd. (includes allowance for outer border and binding)

Light blue: ⅔ yd.

Shadow
Medium orange: ½ yd.

Light orange: ½ yd.

Backing 1¼ yds.

Batting 44" x 44"

*Fabric amount allows for cutting border strips on the lengthwise grain and for ½"-wide bias binding. Cutting borders on the lengthwise grain will help your quilt lie flat. See page 70 in *General Project Guidelines*.

Block Assembly

Block A: Make eight blocks.

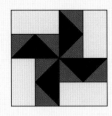

Step 1. Join light blue and dark blue triangles (cut from 2⅞" squares) to make units, then add rectangles as shown. Press.

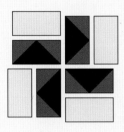

Block B: Make eight blocks.

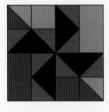

Step 1. Join small light orange and dark orange triangles (cut from 2⅞" squares). Refer to illustration for fabric color changes, then follow the directions for Block A. Press.

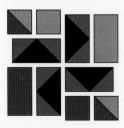

Quilt Top Assembly

Arrange the blocks as shown in the quilt photograph. Sew blocks together in vertical columns, press. Sew the columns together. Press.

Adding Borders

Measure and cut the inner and outer border strips. Refer to the information on pages 70–71 for straight-set corners. Sew the border strips to the quilt top using straight-set corners. Press.

Quilting and Binding

Layer the backing, batting, and top; baste. Outline or stitch-in-the-ditch around the blue and orange pieces. Stipple or use a similar stitch in the background. A simple curved design in the border adds a nice frame. Refer to pages 73–75 for binding information. Attach a hanging sleeve or pocket to the top on the back side of the quilt. Finish by adding your label.

Fire and Ice

Patricia Maixner Magaret

Pullman, Washington, 1999

Machine Quilted by Cheryl Swain

Genesee, Idaho
Quilt Size: 35" x 35"
Block Size: 8" finished

The spotlight focuses on the Shadow pinwheel, giving it a milky, translucent effect. The basic combination is warm/cool with lighter values used in the Shadow.

Fire and Ice

Patricia was inspired by this traditional Pinwheel block design. Although the design looks complicated, only two different blocks were used, making construction less difficult. Patricia wanted to create a transparent look, as if the Shadow was actually a spotlight shining over the quilt, lighting up certain areas. High contrast from light to dark in value heightens this effect.

Fabric Tips

This quilt uses a warm/cool color combination. In order to create the transparent effect, Patricia found two teal colorways of the same print. The lighter version is used in the Shadow and the darker version is in the background. Two different red-orange fabrics were used. The lighter one worked well in the Shadow, and the darker one became part of the individual blocks not covered by the Shadow. Use of the background fabric for the borders helps to keep the design simple and showcases the Shadow. The orange binding nicely frames the completed quilt. Use busy prints with caution as they might interfere with the transparency effect.

Cutting

Refer to page 70 for cutting half- and quarter-square triangles.

All border strips include a few extra inches for length variations. Strips will be cut to the correct length before sewing them to the quilt top.

Background and Border (Dark Teal)
First cut four border strips on the lengthwise grain 2" x 38".

Cut twenty-four 4⅞" squares, then cut in half diagonally.

Cut forty-eight 2⅞" squares, then cut in half diagonally.

Individual Blocks (Dark Red-Orange)
Cut forty-eight pieces using Template 4 (page 108).

Shadow (Light Red-Orange)
Cut sixteen pieces using Template 4 (page 108).

(Light Teal)
Cut eight 4⅞" squares, then cut in half diagonally.

Cut sixteen 2⅞" squares, then cut in half diagonally.

FABRIC REQUIREMENTS

42"-wide fabric. A few extra inches have been included for security, correcting mistakes, and adding to your stash.

Background/Border*
Dark Teal: 1¼ yds. (includes allowance for outer border)

Individual Pinwheels and Binding*
Dark red-orange: 1¼ yds. (includes allowance for binding)

Light red-orange: ¼ yd.

Shadow
Light teal: ½ yd.

Backing 1¼ yds.

Batting 40" x 40"

*Fabric amount allows for cutting border strips on the lengthwise grain and for ½"-wide bias binding. Cutting borders on the lengthwise grain will help your quilt lie flat. See page 70 in *General Project Guidelines*.

Block Assembly

Block A: Make eight.

Step 1. Join two small dark teal triangles (cut from 2⅞" squares) to each of the four dark red-orange parallelograms. Add a large dark teal triangle (cut from 4⅞" squares) to each of these units as shown. Make four of these units and join together to make one block. Press.

Block B: Make eight.

Step 1. Join two small light teal triangles (cut from 2⅞" squares) to one light red-orange parallelogram as shown. Make two units. Press.

Step 2. Join two small dark teal triangles (cut from 2⅞" squares) to one dark red-orange parallelogram as shown. Make two units. Press.

Step 3. Add large triangles (cut from 4⅞" triangles) to these units as shown. Sew units together to form the block.

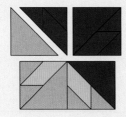

Quilt Assembly

Arrange the blocks as shown in the photograph. Sew in vertical columns, press. Sew the columns together. Press.

Adding Borders

Measure and cut the border strips following the information on pages 70–71 for straight-set corners. Sew to quilt top using straight-set corners. Press.

Quilting and Binding

Layer the backing, batting, and top together; baste. Stitch-in-the-ditch around all dark red-orange shapes. Use a meandering or random quilting design throughout the rest of the quilt. Refer to pages 73–75 for binding information. Attach a hanging sleeve or pocket to the top on the back side of the quilt. Finish by adding your label.

Jewel Box

Interpretation by Donna Ingram Slusser

Pullman, Washington, 1999
Quilt Size: 43" x 43"
Block Size: 8" finished

Jewel Box, original design by Carol Honderich, Goshen, Indiana. Batik and jewel tone fabrics give the traditional Twelve Triangles block a contemporary look. The cool colors of the individual blocks add contrast when placed against the warmer Shadow.

Jewel Box

Carol created this design that uses only three blocks. It adapts well to foundation piecing. The finished quilt can be turned on point for an alternative and interesting effect. The flat red piping appears as a narrow inner border and accents the overall design.

Fabric Tips

This design lends itself to a variety of color combinations and themes. Carol's original plan was to use an assortment of florals to create a beautiful garden-like setting. For her rendition, Donna chose rich jewel-tone colors that reminded her of sparkling precious gems. Using a quilt software program, Donna auditioned a variety of colors and value place ments. She ultimately selected this version for the warm/cool contrast between the Shadow and the individual blocks.

Cutting

Refer to page 70 for cutting half- and quarter-square triangles.

All border strips include a few extra inches for length variations. Strips will be cut to the correct lengths before sewing them to the quilt top.

A template is required for the center square because of its odd size.

Background and Inner Border (Light Green)
First cut four inner border strips on the lengthwise grain: 2" x 40".

Cut fourteen 2⅞" squares, then cut in half diagonally.

Cut fourteen 4⅞" squares, then cut in half diagonally.

Cut six 3¼" squares, then cut in half diagonally twice.

Cut six 5¼" squares, then cut in half diagonally twice.

Individual Blocks and Border (Dark Green)
First cut four border strips on the lengthwise grain: 4½" x 49".

Cut sixteen 5¼" squares, then cut in half diagonally twice.

Individual Blocks (Blue)
Cut sixteen pieces using Template 3 (page 108).

Shadow and Flat Piping (Red)
First cut four strips for the flat piping border on the lengthwise grain: 1¼" x 39".

Cut four 2⅞" squares, then cut in half diagonally.

Cut four 4⅞" squares, then cut in half diagonally.

Cut four 3¼" squares, then cut in half diagonally twice.

Cut four 5¼" squares, then cut in half diagonally twice.

Shadow (Purple)
Cut two 2⅞" squares, then cut in half diagonally.

Cut two 4⅞" squares, then cut in half diagonally.

Cut two 3¼" squares, then cut in half diagonally twice.

Cut two 5¼" squares, then cut in half diagonally twice.

FABRIC REQUIREMENTS

42" wide fabric. A few extra inches have been included for security, correcting mistakes, and for adding to your stash.

Background and Inner Border*
Light green: 1¼ yds. (includes allowance for inner border)

Shadow and Flat Piping
Red: 1¼ yds. (includes allowance for flat piping)
Purple: ¼ yd.

Individual Blocks, Outer Border, and Binding*
Dark Green: 1½ yds. (includes allowance for outer border and binding)

Blue: ½ yd.

Backing 1½ yds.

Batting 47" x 47"

*Fabric amounts allow for cutting border strips and flat piping on the lengthwise grain and for ½"-wide bias binding. Cutting borders on the lengthwise grain will help your quilt lie flat. See page 70 in *General Project Guidelines*.

Block Assembly

Block A: Make four blocks.

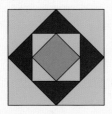

Step 1. Join two light green triangles (cut from 2⅞" squares) to the blue square (Template 4) as shown. Press. Add two more light green triangles (cut from 2⅞" squares). Press.

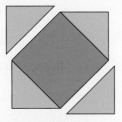

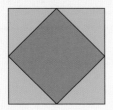

Step 2. Join four dark green triangles (cut from 5¼" squares), using same technique as shown in Step 1. Press. At this point, all outside edges will be bias. Handle with care.

Step 3. Join four light green triangles (cut from 4⅞" squares) as shown in Step 1. Press.

Block B: Make eight blocks.

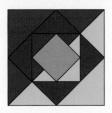

Join the light green and red triangles (cut from 3¼" squares) as shown. Press.

Refer to block illustration for fabric changes, then follow directions for Block A.

Block C: Make four blocks.

Refer to illustration for fabric changes, then follow instructions for Block B.

Quilt Top Assembly

Arrange the blocks as shown in the quilt photograph. Sew together in vertical columns. Press. Sew the columns together. Press.

Adding Borders

Red Flat Piping

Measure and cut the final lengths for the four 1¼" x 41" precut border strips. Refer to the information on pages 70–71. Press each strip in half lengthwise with wrong sides together. Align raw edges of piping strips with raw edges of quilt top and baste together using a scant ¼" seam allowance.

Light Green Border

Measure and cut the final lengths for the four 2" x 40" precut border strips. Refer to the information on pages 70–71 for straight-set corners. Sew to the quilt top using straight-set corners. Press.

Dark Green Border

Measure and cut the final lengths for the four 4¼" x 49" precut dark green border strips. Refer to information on pages 71–72 for mitered corners. Sew the border strips to the quilt top using mitered corners. Press.

Quilting and Binding

Layer the backing, batting, and top; baste. Outline or stitch-in-the-ditch around the blocks and individual triangles and center square. Quilt diagonal lines in the light green background areas. Quilt a decorative stitch in the dark green, purple, and red sections. Refer to pages 73–75 for binding information. Attach a hanging sleeve or pocket to the top on the back side of the quilt. Finish by adding your label.

A Dash Through the Garden

Donna Ingram Slusser
Pullman, Washington, 1999

Kirstin Linnett Nicholson
Seabeck, Washington, 1999
Quilt Size: 76" x 96"
Block Size: 10" finished

A Dash Through the Garden, designed and machine quilted by Donna Ingram Slusser. Top made by Kirstin Linnett Nicholson. Floral prints add understated charm to this design based on the traditional Churn Dash block. To create an open, airy feeling, Donna and Kirstin used the alternate plain block setting, in addition to the omission of partial blocks.

A Dash Through the Garden

This quilt makes good use of the alternate plain block setting to give the design a feeling of open air and spaciousness. The half-blocks in the Shadow layer contribute to the airiness of the design. Designed as a bed-size quilt, this plan can easily be converted to a large wall quilt by omitting the top and bottom row of blocks to make a quilt approximately 76" square. If a smaller quilt is desired, decrease the size of the blocks (for example, to 7 1/2" or 5") to accommodate your needs .

Fabric Tips

Donna and Kirstin created a country garden appearance by using an assortment of floral prints. A combination of plaids would create an equally beautiful quilt with a country flavor. For a more sophisticated appearance, try a palette of batiks or tone-on-tone prints. Or combine just three colors and fabrics for another variation. Let your imagination be your guide!

For a floral garden effect, select thirty-three different fabrics that have medium-size floral motifs on light backgrounds for the individual blocks. Only small amounts are needed of each print. A black floral print created a Victorian feel for both the Shadow and border.

A softly textured print makes up the background. Be sure there is good value contrast between all the design elements.

Cutting

Refer to page 70 for cutting squares for half- and quarter-square triangles.

All border strips include a few extra inches for length variations. Strips will be cut to correct length before sewing to quilt top.

Background (Light)
Cut twenty-six 10½" squares (for the setting blocks).

Cut four 10⅞" squares, then cut in half diagonally.

Cut forty-eight 4⅞" squares, then cut in half diagonally.

Cut ninety-six 2½" x 4½" rectangles.

Individual Blocks
Medium Value Fabric (Florals)
If using one fabric for all of the individual blocks:

Cut sixty-two 4⅞" squares, then cut in half diagonally.

Cut twenty-nine 2½" squares.

Cut four 5¼" squares, then cut in half diagonally twice.

Cut four 2⅞" squares, then cut in half diagonally.

OR

For a scrap floral look, make twenty-nine blocks using a different floral print for each block. For each block from one floral print:

FABRIC REQUIREMENTS

42"-fabric. A few extra inches have been included for security, correcting mistakes and adding to your stash.

Background
Light: 4¼ yds.

Individual Blocks
One medium floral value fabric: 1¾ yds.

OR

For a scrap look, use thirty-three different florals, each 5½" x 14".

Shadow, Border, and Binding*
Black floral: 3⅛ yds. (includes allowance for border and binding)

Backing 6 yds.

Batting 84" x 106"

* Fabric amount allows for cutting-border strips on the lengthwise grain and for ½"-wide bias binding. Cutting borders on the lengthwise grain will help your quilt lie flat. See page 70 in *General Project Guidelines*.

Cut two 4⅞" squares, then cut in half diagonally.

Cut one 2½" square.

Repeat for twenty-nine blocks.

In addition, there are eight Shadow half-blocks. One floral fabric is used to make two of these blocks.

From each floral print:

Cut one 4⅞" square, then cut in half diagonally.

Cut one 5¼" square, then cut in half diagonally twice.

Cut one 2⅞" square, then cut in half diagonally.

Repeat four times for eight blocks.

Shadow and Border (Black Floral)

First cut the border strips on the lengthwise grain. All border strips include a few extra inches for length variations. Strips will be cut to the correct lengths before sewing them to the quilt top.

Cut two strips 4½" x 100".

Cut two strips 4½" x 80".

Cut fourteen 4⅞" squares, then cut in half diagonally.

Cut thirty-six rectangles 2½" x 4½".

Cut four 5¼" squares, then cut in half diagonally twice.

Block Assembly

Block A: Make twenty-four blocks, using a different floral fabric for each block.

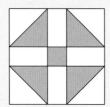

Join pieces together as shown.

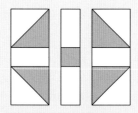

Block B: Make five blocks.

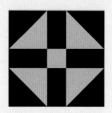

Refer to illustration for fabric changes, then follow directions for Block A.

Block C: Make eight blocks. Use one fabric to make two identical blocks.

Join pieces together as shown.

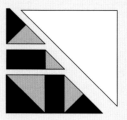

Quilt Top Assembly

Arrange blocks and setting squares as shown in the quilt photograph. Sew blocks together in vertical columns, press. Sew columns together, press.

Adding Borders

Measure and cut the final lengths for the 4½" x 100" and the 4½" x 80" precut border strips following the information for straight-set corners on pages 70–71. Sew to the quilt top using straight-set corners. Press.

Backing

Cut the six yards into two equal lengths. Piece vertically, then press the seam open. To prevent shrinkage, wash the backing before you layer your quilt.

Quilting and Binding

Layer the backing, batting, and top; baste. Outline or stitch-in-the-ditch around the pieces in the individual blocks. Stipple or use a simple stitch in the background and in the Shadow. Refer to pages 73–75 for binding information. Attach a hanging sleeve or pocket to the top on the back side of the quilt. Finish by adding your label.

Rainbow Stars

Lloyd and Donna Slusser

Pullman, Washington, 1999
Quilt Size: 76" x 100"
Block Size: 12" finished

Lloyd handpainted two fabrics for this quilt—
the rainbow fabric and the darker Shadow
fabric. The multicolored rainbow fabric has been
cut into smaller pieces that shimmer and sparkle
throughout the design. The twisted
ribbon border encircles and frames the stars.

Rainbow Stars

Even though this Crystal Star block design looks complicated, it is relatively easy. It uses two simple shapes (triangles and squares) and only two blocks. When the blocks are rotated, the beautiful star Shadow design emerges. The twisted ribbon border effect also uses simple shapes. The center medallion section could stand alone as a large wall quilt if the top and bottom rows of individual stars were omitted. Alternately, make a much smaller wall quilt by simply reducing the block size to nine, eight, or six inches.

Fabric Tips

Lloyd used two of his own hand-painted fabrics to interpret this design (see page 95). One piece, a muted medium blue, has been used for the Shadow. The second is multi-colored, where the paints have been applied to the fabric and allowed to run together. When cut up, no two pieces are alike. The soft, pale blue background fabric is a purchased print that reads as a textured solid from a distance. Even though only three fabrics have been used in this quilt, it looks as if it contains many prints. Since the one fabric is so busy, Lloyd wisely selected two other fabrics that were calm to give the quilt a peaceful, yet lively, colorful look.

This quilt plan would be beautiful in a variety of themes and color schemes. Patriotic would be appropriate; batiks would make it exciting and rich, and plaids and stripes would lend a country feeling.

Cutting

Refer to page 70 for cutting squares to make half-and quarter-square triangles.

All border strips include a few extra inches for length variations. Strips will be cut to the correct length before sewing to the quilt top.

Individual Blocks and Shadow Blocks Background (Light Blue)
First cut border strips on the lengthwise grain.

Inner border

Cut two strips 2½" x 56".

Cut two strips 2½" x 80".

Third border

Cut two strips 4½" x 74".

Cut two strips 4½" x 98".

Cut sixty 3½" squares.

Cut one hundred and fourteen 3⅞" squares, then cut in half diagonally.

Cut six 4¼" squares, then cut in half diagonally twice.

Individual Stars (Rainbow fabric)
Cut one hundred and forty-four 3⅞" squares, then cut in half diagonally.

Shadow (Medium Blue)
First cut the border strips on the lengthwise grain.

Cut two strips 4½" x 82".

Cut two strips 4½" x 106".

FABRIC REQUIREMENTS

42"-wide fabric. A few extra inches have been included for security, correcting mistakes, and adding to your stash.

Background, Inner and Third Border
Light blue: 4 yds.

Shadow, Ribbon Border, Outer Border, and Binding*
Medium blue: 3¾ yds. (includes allowance for border and binding)

Individual Stars and Ribbon Border (Second Border)*
Rainbow fabric: 2½ yds. (includes allowance for pieced border)

Backing 6 yds.

Batting 82" x 106"

*Fabric amounts allow for cutting border strips on the lengthwise grain and for ½"-wide binding. Cutting borders on the lengthwise grain will help your quilt lie flat. See page 70 in *General Project Guidelines*.

Cut twelve 3½" squares.

Cut forty-two 3⅞" squares, then cut in half diagonally.

Cut six 4¼" squares, then cut in half diagonally twice.

Twisted Ribbon Border Background (Light Blue)

Cut two 4⅞" squares, then cut in half diagonally.

Cut sixteen 5¼" squares, then cut in half diagonally twice.

Shadow (Medium Blue)

Cut sixteen 5¼" squares, then cut in half diagonally twice.

(Rainbow)

Cut thirty-four 4⅞" squares, then cut in half diagonally.

Block Assembly

Individual Stars and Shadow

Block A: Make twelve blocks.

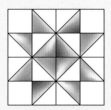

Step 1. Join twelve rainbow triangles to twelve background triangles (cut from 3⅞" squares). Press.

Step 2. Add squares to the units as shown. Press.

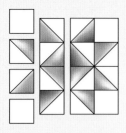

Block B: Make twelve blocks.

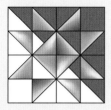

Step 1. Join two background triangles to two Shadow triangles (cut from 4¼" squares). Add one rainbow triangle (cut from 3⅞" square).

Step 2. Refer to block illustration for fabric changes to make units from triangles (cut from 4⅞" squares).

Quilt Top Assembly

Arrange the star blocks as shown in the quilt photograph. Sew blocks together in vertical columns, press. Sew the columns together, press.

Adding the Borders

Inner Border (Light Blue)

Measure and cut the final length for 2½" x 56" and 2½" x 80" precut border strips following the information on pages 70–71. Sew to the quilt top using straight-set corners. Press.

Twisted Ribbon (Second) Border

See instructions on the next page.

Third Border (Background) and Outer Border (Shadow)

The background border strips are joined to the Shadow border strips and sewn to the quilt top as one unit. Refer to the information on pages 71–72 for mitered corners. Measure and cut the final length for the precut border strips.

Background (Light Blue)

Two strips 4½" x 74"
Two strips 4½" x 98"

Shadow Fabric (Medium Blue)

Two strips 4½" x 82"
Two strips 4½" x 106"

Follow the information for mitered corners on pages 71–72. Sew to the quilt top using mitred corners. Press.

Backing

Cut the six yards into two 3 yard lengths. Piece vertically, then press the seam open. To prevent shrinkage, wash the backing before you layer your quilt.

Twisted Ribbon Border Block Assembly

Block Size: 4" finished

Blocks C, D, E
Refer to illustrations for fabric placement and number of each block to make. Small triangles are cut from 5¼" squares. Large triangles are cut from 4⅞" squares.

Block C
Make 60

Block D
Make 4

Block E
Make 4

To complete the border strips, rotate the blocks and join together.

Top Border
Step 1. Join twelve C Blocks. Add one Block D to the right end of the row.

Step 2. Add a Block E to each end of the strip. Press. Sew to the quilt top. Press.

Bottom Border
Step 1. Join twelve C Blocks. Add one Block D to the left end of the row.

Step 2. Add a block E to each end of the strip. Press. Sew to the bottom of the quilt top. Press.

Left Side Border
Join eighteen C Blocks as shown in the quilt photograph. Add one Block D to the top of the column. Press. Sew to left side of quilt top. Press.

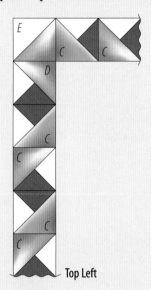

Top Left

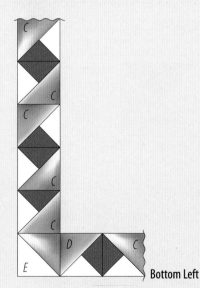

Bottom Left

Right Side Border
Join eighteen C Blocks. Add one Block D to the bottom of the column. Press. Sew to the right side of quilt top. Press.

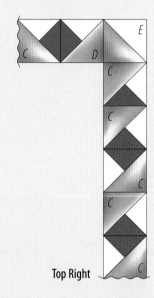

Top Right

Bottom Right

Quilting and Binding

Layer the backing, batting, and top; baste. Because the design tends to be busy, keep the quilting designs simple. The designers recommend outlining the pieces in the main part of the design and in the twisted ribbon border. The inner border has been quilted with straight lines. Use a simple design in the outer borders, similar to the straight lines shown. It provides a nice frame and directs the eye inward. Refer to pages 73–75 for binding information. Attach a hanging sleeve or pocket to the top on the back side of the quilt. Finish by adding your label.

Lloyd Slusser's Handpainted Fabric

Lloyd has been handpainting fabric for garment construction and quilting since 1990. He creates many different one-of-a-kind pieces, as well as some basic designs, such as the Rainbow Fabric used in the quilt, "Rainbow Stars" (page 91). He prefers Versatex™ textile paint because when the process is finished, it is difficult to feel the paint on the fabric surface, giving it a very soft hand (feel). This paint is also easy to heat set and is permanent. If you are interested in painting some of your own fabric, Lloyd's method follows. He also recommends checking out the more detailed information found in several books on painting and dyeing fabric, as well as in the catalogs put out by the suppliers of fabric paints (see Sources, page 109).

Fabric

Lloyd uses good quality, 100% cotton fabric, with no finishes such as permapress. The letters PFD (Prepared for Dyeing) can be found on the end of the bolts of fabric specially prepared for painting and dyeing. He prefers white, bleached cotton because the colors stay true. Off-white, unbleached muslin can also be used to achieve a different color, usually not as bright or intense. Lloyd also paints fabrics referred to as "white-on-white" or "white-on-muslin" prints. These fabrics have a pattern on them that offers some resistance to the paint and creates beautiful texture when the paint is dry.

Fabric Preparation

Cut fabric into manageable pieces for painting. Lloyd uses 36" x 42" pieces, but any smaller size can be used. Wash the fabrics in the machine before painting. Keep them damp until used.

Supplies

Versatex™ Textile Paint

Water, for thinning paints and cleaning brushes

Containers for thinning and mixing paint (such as cottage cheese or dessert topping cartons, etc.). Do not re-use these containers for food preparation or storage.

Paint Brushes, 1" to 3" wide

Clear Plastic Sheets, approx. 3" larger on all sides than the fabric pieces

Iron, for heat setting fabrics

Lloyd's Method for Painting Fabric

Lloyd uses a wet-on-wet method, which means that wet paint is applied to the dampened, wet fabric.

Step 1. Tape a clear plastic sheet to a flat table surface. (Place newspapers under the plastic if desired.)

Step 2. Lay a damp piece of fabric on the plastic.

Step 3. Place a small amount of Versatex paint in a container. Thin with water to the consistency of half-and-half cream.

Step 4. Paint the fabric. Use one or many colors. Notice how the colors run together and blend, creating interesting effects. Some paints can also be mixed in the containers if desired.

Step 5. Let the fabric dry completely.

Step 6. Heat set by pressing the fabric with a hot, dry iron.

Step 7. Wash, dry, and press the fabric.

Use and enjoy!

Autumn Leaves:
A Shadow Quilt

Ellis R. Farny
La Mirada, California, 1998
Quilt Size: 48" x 48"
Block Size: 7 ½" finished

Ellis says, "I have been collecting fall colored
fabrics for some time, awaiting the right pattern.
This design technique was exactly right."

Autumn Leaves: A Shadow Quilt

Ellis used the simple leaf pattern to create a stunning design. Only a few of the leaves twist and turn, but the overall effect is one of motion. Contrasting values and textures in the various borders gives the piece a beautiful frame. This quilt has seven different blocks, but they use simple shapes, making construction fairly easy.

Fabric Tips

Ellis chose a richly textured, dark green print for the Shadow that adds life to the area without being too busy. She used an assortment of leaf-textured prints in a wide range of values that are mostly calm. What a wonderful way to showcase a collection of theme prints. Notice that some of the leaves are similar in value to the background. This adds mystery and intrigue to the viewer's eye. The narrow inner borders are shaded from light to dark to create depth. The multicolor fabric border pulls the many colors and textures together. If you do not have a collection of leaf fabrics, directions are given for using only one fabric for the individual leaves.

Cutting

Refer to page 70 for cutting half-square triangles.

Background (Light)
Cut forty-seven 2⅜" squares, then cut in half diagonally.

Cut one 3⅞" square, then cut in half diagonally.

Cut nineteen 2" squares.

Cut thirteen 3½" squares.

Cut thirty-seven 2" x 3½" rectangles.

Shadow (Green)
Cut thirty-eight 2⅜" squares, then cut in half diagonally.

Cut one 3⅞" square, then cut in half diagonally.

Cut sixteen 2" squares.

Cut ten 3½" squares.

Cut twenty-eight 2" x 3½" rectangles.

FABRIC REQUIREMENTS

42"-wide fabric. A few extra inches have been included for security, correcting mistakes, and adding to your stash.

Background
Light: 1 yd.

Shadow
Green: ¾ yd.

Individual Leaf Blocks
Twenty-five leaf fabrics:
10" x 10" of each fabric

Or one fabric: 1⅛ yd.

Borders and Binding*

Inner Border
Pale Light Gold: approximately 6" x 42", cut on the lengthwise grain.

Second Border
Dark Gold: approximately 7" x 45", cut on the lengthwise grain.

Third Border
Dark Red-Orange: approximately 6" x 47", cut on the lengthwise grain.

Outer Border and Binding
Multicolor leaf print: 1½ yds.

Backing 2⅞ yds.

Batting 52" x 52"

*Fabric amount allows for cutting border strips on the lengthwise grain and for ½"-wide bias binding. Cutting borders on the lengthwise grain will help your quilt lie flat. See page 70 in *General Project Guidelines*.

Individual Blocks (Leaves)

Instructions are for one block. Repeat for twenty-five blocks.

Cut one 3½" x 5" rectangle.

Cut one 2" x 3½" rectangle.

Cut three 2⅜" squares, then cut in half diagonally.

Borders

All border strips include a few extra inches for length variations. Each strip will be sized to the correct length before sewing to the quilt top.

First Inner Border (Pale Gold)

Cut four strips on the lengthwise grain 1" x 42".

Second Border (Dark Gold)

Cut four strips on the lengthwise grain 1¼" x 45".

Third Border (Dark Red-Orange)

Cut four strips on the lengthwise grain 1" x 47".

Outer Border and Binding (Multicolor Leaf print)

Cut two strips on the lengthwise grain 4" x 49".

Cut two strips on the lengthwise grain 4" x 52".

Use the remainder of the fabric for binding.

Block Assembly

Block A: Make eleven blocks using a different fabric for each leaf.

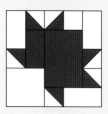

Instructions are for one individual block.

Step 1. Join six background triangles and six leaf triangles (cut from 2⅜" squares). Press.

Step 2. Add squares and rectangles and join together as shown. Press.

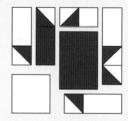

Blocks B, C, D, E, and F
For remaining blocks, refer to the illustrations for fabric changes. Use a different fabric for each leaf.

Step 1. Block B: Refer to illustration for fabric changes, then follow directions for Block A.

Step 2. Blocks C, D, E, and F: Join a background triangle and a Shadow triangle (cut from 2⅜" squares). Press. Make two units for each block.

Step 3. Blocks E and F: Join two background triangles to two Shadow fabric triangles (cut from 3⅞" squares). Press. Make two units, one for each block.

Step 4. Follow directions for Block A to complete blocks.

Block B
Make 8

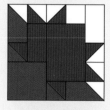

Block C
Make 2

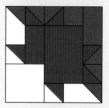

Block D
Make 2

Block E
Make 1

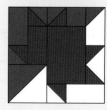

Block F
Make 1

Quilt Top Assembly

Arrange blocks as shown in the quilt photograph. Sew blocks together in vertical columns, press. Sew the columns together, press.

Adding Borders

Measure and cut the final lengths for each of the precut border strips. Refer to the information on pages 70–71 for straight-set corners. Sew each border to the quilt top in order, using straight-set corners. Press.

Quilting and Binding

Layer the backing, batting, and top together; baste. Outline or stitch in the ditch around the leaves and Shadow. Gentle curved lines in the background give the feeling of air currents. Refer to pages 73–75 for binding information. Attach a hanging sleeve or pocket to the top on the back side of the quilt. Finish by adding your label.

A beautiful border was created with a variety of textures and contrasting values.

Pinwheels Spinning

Designed and machine quilted by Donna Ingram Slusser

Pullman, Washington, 1999

Top made by Kirstin Linnett Nicholson

Seabeck, Washington, 1999

Quilt Size: 50" x 50"

Block Size: 8" finished

An assortment of plaids gives this design a homespun appearance. Each Pinwheel block contains two different plaids, contributing to the illusion of motion.

Pinwheels Spinning

Donna has always loved this pinwheel design; she began the design for this quilt by drawing an arrangement with small pinwheels in every block. The effect was too busy and the Shadow was lost. An alternate plain block setting opened up the design and solved the problem. This rendition makes a nice wall quilt, but could easily be adapted to fit a bed by adding additional rows of pinwheels to the top, bottom, and sides. An assortment of plaids gives this version a heartwarming, homespun feeling. Donna wanted a homespun, scrappy look, so she dipped into her scrap bag to find many different plaids. A palette of batiks would give a sophisticated, contemporary look. Another option could use a limited number of colors and fabrics—one for the background, two for the Shadow, and two for the individual blocks.

FABRIC REQUIREMENTS

42"-wide fabric. A few extra inches have been included for security, correcting mistakes, and adding to your stash.

Background and Inner Border
Light tan: 2 yds.

Shadow and Binding*
Blue: ⅝ yd.

Red: 1½ yds. (includes allowance for binding)

Individual Blocks
Assorted scraps OR
Light fabric: ¾ yd.
Dark fabric: ¾ yd.

Outer Border*
Medium Green: 1½yds.

Dark Green: 1½yds.

Backing 2¼ yds.

Batting 54" x 54"

*Fabric amount allows for cutting border strips on lengthwise grain and for ½"-wide bias binding. Cutting borders on the lengthwise grain will help your quilt lie flat. See page 70 in *General Project Guidelines*.

Fabric Tips

Keep the busy/calm effect of the individual fabrics in mind when selecting your colors and prints. Value also plays an important role. The two Shadow fabrics in this version are medium-dark and fairly calm. They provide a nice backdrop for the individual blocks without being overwhelming. If you wish to create a scrap quilt as shown, remember that value is very important. There must be light and dark contrast between the pieces so the different design elements (Shadow and individual pinwheels) can be seen. Notice that each small pinwheel also uses one calm fabric and one busier fabric.

Cutting

Refer to page 70 for cutting half- and quarter-square triangles.

All border strips include a few extra inches for length variations. Strips will be cut to the correct length before sewing them to the quilt top.

Template 1 (page 108) is "directional." Be sure the template is always right side up. Fabric must also be right side up. For quick cutting, stack fabric in layers with each layer right side facing up.

A template is also required for the parallelogram because of its odd size.

Cut four inner border strips 1½" x 50".

Cut twenty-four pieces using Template 1 (page 108).

Cut four pieces using Template 2 (page 108).

Cut eight 5¼" squares, then cut in half diagonally twice.

Cut eight 8½" squares (four squares are setting blocks.)

Individual Blocks

Small Pinwheels: Instructions are for one block. Repeat for 13 blocks.

(Light Fabric)

Cut two 3⅞" squares. Cut in half diagonally.

(Dark Fabric)

Cut one 5¼" square, then cut in half diagonally twice.

Shadow (Blue)

Cut twelve Template 1 (page 108).

Cut two 5¼" squares, then cut in half diagonally twice.

Cut four 4½" x 8½" rectangles.

Shadow (Red)

Cut twelve pieces using Template 1 (page 108).

Cut four 4½" squares.

Cut two 1⅞" squares, then cut in half diagonally.

Cut three 5¼" squares, then cut in half diagonally twice.

Cut four 4½" x 8½" rectangles.

Outer Borders
(Medium Green)

Cut two strips on the lengthwise grain 4½" x 53".

(Dark Green)

Cut two strips on the lengthwise grain 4½" x 53".

Block Assembly

Small pinwheels use a light green and dark green for illustration and placement purposes.

Block A: Make four blocks.

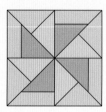

Step 1. Join one dark plaid triangle (cut from 5¼" square) and one background triangle (cut from 5¼" square) as shown. Press.

Join Template 1 and a light plaid triangle (cut from a 3⅞" square) as illustrated. Sew together to make one unit. Make four units. Press.

Step 2. Sew four units together to make one block. Press.

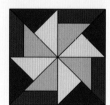

Blocks B and C

For Blocks B and C, refer to illustrations for fabric changes, then follow directions for Block A.

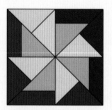

Block B
Make 4

Block C
Make 1

Block D: Make four blocks.

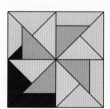

Join a red triangle (cut from 1⅞" square) and a Template 2 (page 108) piece as shown. Refer to the illustration for fabric changes, then follow the directions for Block A.

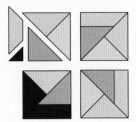

Block E: Make four blocks.

Join a red rectangle 4½" x 8½" and a blue rectangle 4½" x 8½" as shown. Press.

Block F: Make four blocks.

Step 1. Mark a diagonal line from corner to corner on the back side of a 4½" red square.

Step 2. Align the 4½" square on one corner of an 8½" background square with right sides together. Sew on the line. Press newly formed triangle shape back and trim away extra layers.

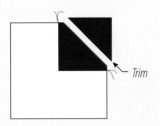

Trim

Block G
Use four blocks cut 8½" x 8½" from background fabric as setting blocks.

Quilt Top Assembly

Arrange the blocks as shown in the following plan. Rotate when necessary to match the quilt photograph. Sew blocks together in vertical columns. Press. Sew the columns together. Press.

A	F	D	G	A
G	B	E	B	F
D	E	C	E	D
F	B	E	B	G
A	G	D	F	A

Adding Borders

Inner Border

Measure and cut the final lengths for the four 1½" x 50" precut border strips. Refer to the information on pages 70–71 for straight-set corners. Sew the border strips to the quilt top, using straight-set corners. Press.

Outer Border

Measure and cut the final lengths for the two 4½" x 53" precut dark green and two 4½" x 53" precut medium green border strips. Refer to information on pages 71–72 for mitered corners. Sew border strips to quilt top using mitered corners. Press.

Quilting and Binding

Layer the backing, batting, and top; baste. Outline or stitch-in-the-ditch around the small pinwheel pieces. Stipple or use a simple stitch in the Shadow and background. Refer to pages 73–75 for binding information. Attach a hanging sleeve or pocket to the top on the back side of the quilt. Finish by adding your label.

Passing Through

Designed and pieced by Patricia Maixner Magaret

Pullman, Washington, 1999

Machine quilted by Cheryl Swain

Genesee, Idaho
Quilt Size: 41" x 41"
Block Size: 8" finished

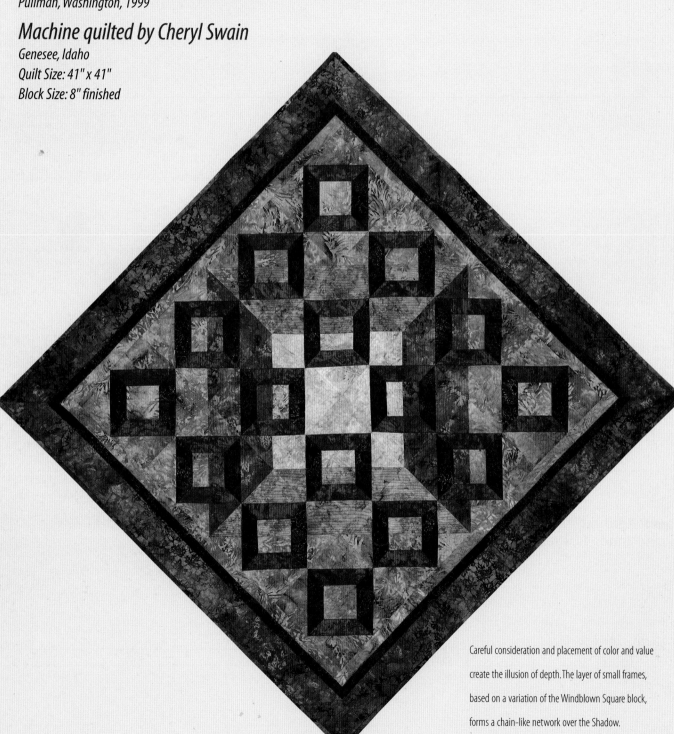

Careful consideration and placement of color and value create the illusion of depth. The layer of small frames, based on a variation of the Windblown Square block, forms a chain-like network over the Shadow.

Passing Through

The traditional Windblown Square block was Patricia's original inspiration. She simplified it to create the look of dimensional frames. Working with a draw program on her computer, Patricia explored many variations, oftentimes omitting some of the blocks. Her ultimate goal was to create the subtle illusion of a passageway. When this plan appeared on the screen, she knew this was the one! Notice how the quilting lines accentuate the illusion of depth.

FABRIC REQUIREMENTS

42"-wide fabric. A few extra inches have been included for security, correcting mistakes and adding to your stash.

Background and Inner Border

Light Tan: ¼ yd.

Dark Tan: 1¼ yds. (includes allowance for first inner border)

Individual Blocks and Middle Border

Light Magenta: ½ yd.

Dark Magenta: 1¼ yds. (includes allowance for middle border)

Shadow, Outer Border and Binding*

Light Teal: ½ yd.

Dark Teal: 1½ yds. (includes allowance for outer border and binding)

Backing 1¼ yds.

Batting 45" x 45"

*Fabric amount allows for cutting border strips on the lengthwise grain and for ½"-wide bias binding. Cutting borders on the lengthwise grain will help your quilt lie flat. See page 70 in *General Project Guidelines*.

Fabric Tips

A warm/cool color combination gives the necessary contrast to this design. Two different values of magenta were used in the small frames. They are positioned on top of the Shadow, made in two tones of teal. The background is composed of a light tan in the center area and a darker tan on the outside. This creates the effect of light coming from behind the Shadow. Patricia used a palette of batiks for their dappled effect that looks solid from a distance, yet gives the appearance of smeared colors and texture. The batiks are a good choice for the contemporary, sophisticated look. Caution: Be careful if using busy prints as they may detract from the illusion of depth.

Cutting

Refer to page 70 for cutting half- and quarter-square triangles.

All border strips include a few extra inches for length variations. Strips will be cut to correct length before sewing to quilt top.

Templates are used for some pieces because of their odd sizes.

Background (Light Tan)

Cut four pieces using Template 6 (page 108).

Cut two 4⅞" squares, then cut in half diagonally.

Cut two 5¼" squares, then cut in half diagonally twice.

Background and Border (Dark Tan)

First cut four inner border strips on the lengthwise grain 1½" x 36".

Cut four pieces using Template 3 (page 108).

Cut eight pieces using Template 6 (page 108).

Cut twelve 4⅞" squares, then cut in half diagonally.

Cut four 5¼" squares, then cut in half diagonally twice.

Shadow and Outer Border (Dark Teal)

First cut four outer border strips on the lengthwise grain 3¼" x 45".

Cut six pieces using Template 6 (page 108).

Cut three 4⅞" squares, then cut in half diagonally.

Cut three 5¼" squares, then cut in half diagonally twice.

Shadow (Light Teal)

Cut six pieces using Template 6 (page 108).

Cut three 4⅞" squares, then cut in half diagonally.

Cut three 5¼" squares, then cut in half diagonally twice.

Individual Blocks and Border (Dark Magenta)

First cut four border strips on the lengthwise grain 1¼" x 37".

Cut thirty-two frames using Template 5 (page 108). Mark the intersection points onto the wrong side of the fabric.

(Light Magenta)

Cut thirty-two frames using Template 5. Mark the intersection points onto the wrong side of the fabric.

Block Assembly

Block A: Make four.

Step 1. Sew a large dark tan triangle (cut from 4⅞" squares) to two dark magenta and two light magenta frames as shown. Press.

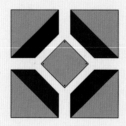

Step 2. Sew four frames to a center dark tan square as shown. Stitch from one intersection point to the next. Backtack at both ends. Check that dark frames are across from each other, and light frames are across from each other. Press.

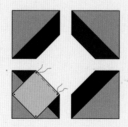

Step 3. Stitch the four short seams of the frames together, starting from the outside edge of the block and going only to the intersection "dot" as shown. Backtack. Press.

Blocks B, C, D, and E

For remaining blocks, refer to illustrations for fabric changes.

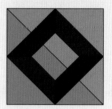

Block B
Make 4

Block C
Make 4

Block D
Make 2

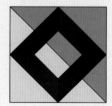

Block E
Make 2

Block Construction

Step 1. Make pieced corner units. Sew small triangles (cut from 5¼" square) together.

Step 2. Sew two rectangles together to make a center square. Refer to illustrations for fabric selection.

Step 3. Refer to directions for Block A to finish.

Quilt Top Assembly

Arrange the blocks as shown in the quilt photograph. Sew blocks together in vertical columns. Press. Sew the columns together. Press.

Adding Borders

Measure and cut length for border strips following information on pages 70–71. Sew to quilt top using mitered corners following information on pages 71-72. Press.

Quilting and Binding

Layer the backing, batting, and top together; baste. Quilt-in-the-ditch around the individual frames. Use close straight-line quilting in the Shadow, and use a meandering or random quilting design in the background. Refer to pages 73–75 for binding information. Finish by adding your label.

A combination of quilting techniques adds to the texture and overall design of the quilt.

Templates

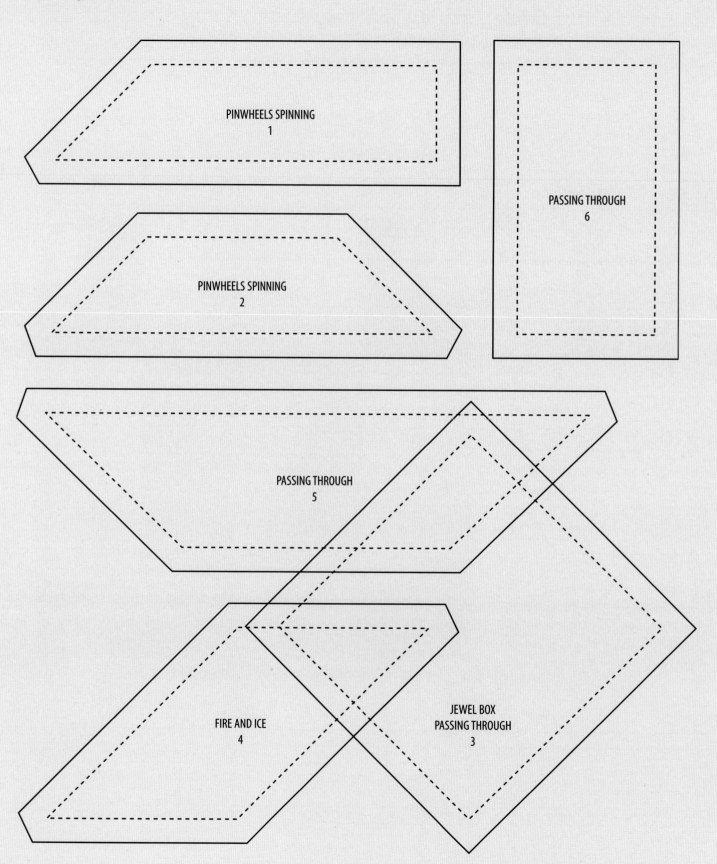

PINWHEELS SPINNING
1

PINWHEELS SPINNING
2

PASSING THROUGH
6

PASSING THROUGH
5

FIRE AND ICE
4

JEWEL BOX
PASSING THROUGH
3

Sources

The following patterns are available from Patricia and Donna's Forget-Me-Not Studio:
A Tisket a Tasket
Autumn Accents
Blue Plane Special
Celestial Encore
Cosmic Conflict
Mantilla for Mom
My Cup of Tea
Phantom Fleet
Sew This Is What Quilting Is All About

Forget-Me-Not Studio
Patricia Magaret and Donna Slusser
P.O. Box 841
Pullman, WA 99163

Forget-Me-Not Studio is our pattern company! Visit our web site at www.forgetmenotstudio.com for updates about our latest patterns, happenings, a gallery of quilt photos, teaching and lecture information, travel schedule, and all kinds of fun and tidbits.

A pattern for a quilt similar to Kimono Secrets is available from:
The Calico Basket
550 Main Street - #A
Edmonds, WA 98020
1-800-720-6446
calicob@ix.netcom.com
www.calicobasket.com

Steam-A-Seam 2® is a product of Warm Products, Inc. Ask for it at your favorite quilt shop.

Versatex™ Textile Paint can be obtained from Dharma Trading Company, Box 150916, San Rafael, CA 94915. 1-800-542-5227.

We love to see and hear about projects inspired by the book. Send us your photos and comments.

Subject Index

Alternate plain block setting, 40
Asymmetrical blocks, 44–46
Basic block, choosing, 12
Binding, 73–75
Block sizes, using multiple, 12, 46–47
Borders
    extending blocks into, 49–51
    measuring for, 70
    mitered, 71–72
    straight-set, 70–71
Color inspiration, 34–37
Computer, designing on, 63–67
Contrast, 25–34
Design, multi-layer, 10
Designing Shadow quilts, 17–22
    blocks that can be used, 23
    supplies needed, 20
Drawing software, 66–67
Fabric requirements, general, 69
Fabrics, choosing, 25–37
Grain, 69

Grid system for blocks, 14, 17
Half-square triangles, cutting, 70
Handpainting fabric, 95
Hanging sleeve, 75
Individual blocks layer, drawing, 21
Labels, 75
Layers, planning, 20, 46–47
Mock-ups, 27, 28, 30, 33
    making, 57–61
    value scale, 26
Offset blocks, 49
Planning process, 20
Pressing, 69
Print design contrast, 31–32
Projects
    A Dash Through the Garden,
        88–90
    Autumn Leaves, 96–99
    Fire and Ice, 82–84
    Jewel Box, 85–87
    Passing Through, 104–107

Pinwheels Spinning, 100–103
Rainbow Stars, 91–95
Shadow Play, 79–81
Shoo-Fly Don't Bother Me, 76–78
Quarter-square triangles, cutting, 70
Seam allowance, 69
Shadow layer, 9, 10, 13–14, 19
    drawing, 22
Shapes in blocks, 17–18
Software for quilt design, 64–67
Space, positive and negative, 18–19
Symmetrical block arrangements,
    41, 42
Temperature contrast, 28–31
Theme, relating blocks by, 12, 55
Tools, 39
Transparent effect, 13, 52–54
Triangles, no-template cutting, 70
Value contrast, 25–27
Variations on themes, 39–55

Quilt Index

A Dash Through the Garden, 88
Arcturas, 19
A Tisket a Tasket, 13
Autumn Accents, 8
Autumn Leaves: A Shadow Quilt,
    96
Blue Plane Special, 35
Celestial Encore, 47
Churning Out the Blues, 36
Cosmic Caper, 66
Dawn Shadows, 31
Diana's Star, 45
Echoes of Winter, 51
Escargot's Escapade, 50
Fire and Ice, 82
Fireworks, 37
Forest for the Trees, 10
Ghost Baskets, 45
Glorious Iris, 15

Hot Summer Day at Donna's, 61
I Never Saw a Purple Bear, 18
I Want to See Stars, 29
Intrigue, 26
Jewel Box, 85
Kimono Keepsake, 62
Mantilla for Mom, 16
Mosaic Star, 15
My Cup of Tea, 12
My Little Neck of the Woods, 32
Now I See Stars, 29
Passing Through, 104
Peace and Plenty, 38
Phantom Fleet, 43
Pinwheels Spinning, 100
Pinwheels...wheels...wheels, 4
Purple Passions, 60
Rainbow Stars, 91
Road to the Sunset, 33

Seahorse Cotillion, 48
Second Growth Forest, 59
Sew This Is What Quilting Is All
    About, 68
Shadow Pinwheel, 56
Shadow Play, 79
Shoo Fly Don't Bother Me, 76
Shoo Fly from Outer Space, 20
Star Shadows, 44
The Dove, 43
The Truth Is on the Inside, 24
Tie a Yellow Ribbon, 58
Too Many Stars, 11
Triple Tropical Fruit, 14
Tulips Abound, 54
Twilight Shadows, 30
Untitled 5, 11
Whirligig Awhirl, 52
Winter's Night, 34

About
The Authors

Patricia and Donna both started as traditional quilt-makers in the early 1980s after a lifetime of sewing and crafting. They soon branched out from tradition and began experimenting with color and design. They each began taking familiar blocks and using them in unique and innovative ways. In 1987 they added team-teaching to their friendship. Each brings different views and techniques to almost every subject and method. Patricia is methodical, organized, prefers to design on graph paper, and is known for her beautiful hand quilting. Donna uses the "what would happen if I tried..." method, experimenting with the hands-on approach to fabric and design, and is a machine quilter. Yet underlying all their differences is a common commitment to good workmanship. Their differences have been one of their greatest strengths. Patricia and Donna teach a variety of workshops that appeal to a wide audience of quilt-makers. These classes challenge each person to appreciate their own unique creative gifts. Living in eastern Washington state, these two quiltmakers find the seasonal changes of their surroundings a constant source of inspiration. Their love of music and nature, particularly flowers, is often reflected in their quilts.

Donna Slusser

Patricia Maqaut

Bibliography

McDowell, Ruth B. *Pattern on Pattern: Spectacular Quilts from Traditional Blocks*, Gualala, Calif: Quilt Digest Books, 1991.

In *Pattern on Pattern* Ruth B. McDowell creates beautiful quilts with visually complex patterns made from traditional blocks.

Other Fine Books From C&T Publishing

Art & Inspirations: Ruth B. McDowell, Ruth B. McDowell

The Art of Classic Quiltmaking, Harriet Hargrave and Sharyn Craig

At Home with Patrick Lose: Colorful Quilted Projects, Patrick Lose

Basic Seminole Patchwork, Cheryl Greider Bradkin

Color From the Heart: Seven Great Ways to Make Quilts with Colors You Love, Gai Perry

Curves in Motion: Quilt Designs & Techniques, Judy B. Dales

Deidre Scherer: Work in Fabric & Thread, Deidre Scherer

Easy Pieces: Creative Color Play with Two Simple Blocks, Margaret Miller

Everything Flowers: Quilts from the Garden, Jean and Valori Wells

Exploring Machine Trapunto: New Dimensions, Hari Walner

Fabric Shopping with Alex Anderson, Seven Projects to Help You: Make Successful Choices, Build Your Confidence, Add to Your Fabric Stash, Alex Anderson

Fantastic Fabric Folding: Innovative Quilting Projects, Rebecca Wat

Forever Yours: Wedding Quilts, Clothing & Keepsakes, Amy Barickman

Freddy's House: Brilliant Color in Quilts, Freddy Moran

Free Stuff for Collectors on the Internet, Judy Heim and Gloria Hansen

Free Stuff for Crafty Kids on the Internet, Judy Heim and Gloria Hansen

Free Stuff for Gardeners on the Internet, Judy Heim and Gloria Hansen

Free Stuff for Quilters on the Internet, 2nd Ed., Judy Heim and Gloria Hansen

Free Stuff for Sewing Fanatics on the Internet, Judy Heim and Gloria Hansen

Free Stuff for Stitchers on the Internet, Judy Heim and Gloria Hansen

From Fiber to Fabric: The Essential Guide to Quiltmaking Textiles, Harriet Hargrave

Hand Quilting with Alex Anderson: Six Projects for Hand Quilters, Alex Anderson

Heirloom Machine Quilting, Third Edition, Harriet Hargrave

Make Any Block Any Size, Joen Wolfrom

Mastering Machine Appliqué, Harriet Hargrave

Mastering Quilt Marking: Marking Tools & Techniques, Choosing Stencils, Matching Borders & Corners, Pepper Cory

Michael James: Art & Inspirations, Michael James

The New England Quilt Museum Quilts: Featuring the Story of the Mill Girls. With Instructions for 5 Heirloom Quilts, Jennifer Gilbert

The New Sampler Quilt, Diana Leone

On the Surface: Thread Embellishment & Fabric Manipulation, Wendy Hill

Patchwork Persuasion: Fascinating Quilts from Traditional Designs, Joen Wolfrom

The Photo Transfer Handbook: Snap It, Print It, Stitch It!, Jean Ray Laury

Pieced Flowers, Ruth B. McDowell

Pieced Roman Shades: Turn Your Favorite Quilt Patterns into Window Hangings, Terrell Sundermann

Piecing: Expanding the Basics, Ruth B. McDowell

Plaids & Stripes: The Use of Directional Fabrics in Quilts, Roberta Horton

Quilt It for Kids; 11 Projects, Sports, Fantasy & Animal Themes; Quilts for Children of All Ages, Pam Bono

Quilts for Fabric Lovers, Alex Anderson

Quilts from Europe, Projects and Inspiration, Gül Laporte

Quilts, Quilts, and More Quilts! Diana McClun and Laura Nownes

Recollections, Judith Baker Montano

Rotary Cutting with Alex Anderson: Tips, Techniques, and Projects, Alex Anderson

Rx for Quilters: Stitcher-Friendly Advice for Every Body, Susan Delaney Mech, M.D.

Say It with Quilts, Diana McClun and Laura Nownes

Scrap Quilts: The Art of Making Do, Roberta Horton

Simply Stars: Quilts that Sparkle, Alex Anderson

Six Color World: Color, Cloth, Quilts & Wearables, Yvonne Porcella

Skydyes: A Visual Guide to Fabric Painting, Mickey Lawler

Small Scale Quiltmaking: Precision, Proportion, and Detail, Sally Collins

Soft-Edge Piecing, Jinny Beyer

Special Delivery Quilts, Patrick Lose

Start Quilting with Alex Anderson: Six Projects for First-Time Quilters, Alex Anderson

Through the Garden Gate: Quilters and Their Gardens, Jean and Valori Wells

Tradition with a Twist: Variations on Your Favorite Quilts, Blanche Young and Dalene Young Stone

Trapunto by Machine, Hari Walner

Travels with Peaky and Spike: Doreen Speckmann's Quilting Adventures, Doreen Speckmann

The Visual Dance: Creating Spectacular Quilts, Joen Wolfrom

Wild Birds: Designs for Appliqué & Quilting, Carol Armstrong

Wildflowers: Designs for Appliqué & Quilting, Carol Armstrong

Women of Taste: A Collaboration Celebrating Quilt Artists and Chefs, Girls, Inc.

Yvonne Porcella: Art & Inspirations, Yvonne Porcella

For more information write for a free catalog:
C&T Publishing, Inc.
P.O. Box 1456
Lafayette, CA 94549
(800) 284-1114
e-mail: ctinfo@ctpub.com
http://www.ctpub.com

For quilting supplies:
Cotton Patch Mail Order
3405 Hall Lane, Dept. CTB
Lafayette, CA 94549
(800) 835-4418
(925) 283-7883
e-mail: quiltusa@yahoo.com
http://www.quiltusa.com